Behaviour and misbehaviour

explanations and non-explanations

Behaviour
and misbehaviour

explanations and non-explanations

Nigel Walker

BASIL BLACKWELL · OXFORD

British Library Cataloguing in Publication Data

Walker, Nigel, b. 1917
    Behaviour and misbehaviour : explanations
    and non-explanations.
    Bibl. — Index.
    ISBN 0-631-17810-4
    1. Title
    128   BD450
    Human behaviour

Printed in Great Britain
by Western Printing Services Ltd, Bristol
Bound by The Pitman Press, Bath

Contents

Preface

This book is chiefly concerned with the relationship between expected and unexpected behaviour, and especially those varieties of the latter which psychiatrists tend to call 'abnormal' and sociologists 'deviant'. I have chosen a third name for it, partly in order to preserve my social distance from both disciplines (if discipline is not too strong a term), partly because I really am talking about a concept which is not the exact equivalent of either abnormality or deviance, as will become clear in the chapter on surprise.

One of the main points of the book is to question the traditional positivist's assumption that misbehaviour must always be explained in the same scientific way as behavior. Since I am not anti-positivist I believe that it sometimes has to be, but by no means always; indeed, that scientific explanation—at least as I define it—is sometimes quite inappropriate.

On the other hand, another of my aims is to discuss what form a scientific explanation must or may take, especially one which is about human actions. I hope this part of the book is less tedious than it sounds. Certainly it is necessary, because not only many social scientists but also some philosophers of social science try to impose on the social sciences a rigour which is seldom achieved even by physics.

Again, while both scientists and philosophers of science talk a great deal about 'models', the concept is a vague one, and getting vaguer as its popularity increases. The distinction between models in the mathematical sense, and the 'mechanisms' and analogies which are often pretentiously called 'models', together with the realisation that analogies are neither verifiable nor falsifiable, are crucial for the social sciences. Hence the space devoted to them in Chapters 6 and 7.

Equally necessary, I am afraid, are the discussions of non-explanations. For some reason the study of misbehaviour has generated, in a relatively short period, a remarkable number of bizarre fallacies. Some of these are new. Some are revivals of old performances: Aristotle rides again and yet again in Chapter 4. Even if this book does not succeed in converting many sociologists of deviance to a particular point of view, it may at least convince them that they have something to learn from some philosophers of science.

Almost as important as the fallacies of criminological sociologists or psychologists are their neuroses and obsessions. One is anxiety lest their explanatory hypotheses turn out to have no social utility: hence the discussion of instrumentalism in Chapter 1. As for obsessions, the best example is the eternal quest for what I have called 'the criminologist's stone'—a monolithic 'general theory' which will explain all forms of crime, or even all forms of deviance; and this is discussed in the last chapter.

Another issue which must be faced by any book of this kind is whether the whole attempt to apply science to human actions is misconceived. Those who argue this tend to equate science with explanation, and to overlook its *descriptive* aims. It is possible to argue that actions cannot be described in the way in which science describes inanimate phenomena; but hardly possible to argue that they cannot be grouped into categories (such as 'greetings', 'games of chess', 'insults') or that their frequencies cannot be estimated. But what the anti-positivists are usually attacking is scientific *explanation* of meaningful behaviour. Even here, however, there is sometimes a failure to distinguish the assertion that scientific explanations are inadequate from the assertion that they are inappropriate: hence the discussions in Chapters 8 and 9.

Finally, not enough attention has been paid, even by philosophers of science, to the task of defining what it is one is trying to explain. Durkheim, Sutherland and Albert Cohen were aware that this raises problems, but did not define them, let alone solve them. It may seem odd to reserve these problems for later chapters; but the reason for doing so will become clear by the time they are reached.

Acknowledgements

I would like to record my thanks to

Miss Barbara Allen, my former research assistant, who helped me to review the literature on explanations of crime and deviance in 1972–3, when I started this book;

The Home Office, who provided the grant which enabled me to have her assistance;

Miss Amanda Younie and Miss Deborah Pull, who not only typed the first and second drafts but also drew my attention to many examples of my carelessness;

Miss Rosina Perry and Miss Kirsty Anderson at the Radzino-wicz Library, who helped me to trace some of the less readily available publications to which I have referred.

1 Why explain?

To begin by asking 'Why do we want explanations?' may seem to be carrying thoroughness to a tedious extreme. But the possible answers have important consequences, as the later chapters will demonstrate. In particular, they will determine what is or is not acceptable as an explanation.

EXPLANATION AND CURIOSITY

The commonsense answer is Professor Braithwaite's. An explanation is 'any answer to a "why" question which in any way answers the question, and thereby gives some degree of intellectual satisfaction to the questioner'. The usual reason for asking for an explanation of something is that we are surprised by it: it is unexpected. This is especially true of human behaviour. Unless we are scientists we do not ask why people eat, sleep, play games, make love or read newspapers, although we may ask why someone *doesn't* eat, sleep, play games, make love or read a newspaper. What arouses our everyday curiosity is the departure of people or events from what we expect. Law-breaking is only one example of this: but not all law-breaking. Illegal parking for instance, is so frequent that we are surprised only by someone who parks illegally in front of a police station or traffic warden.

I said 'unless we are scientists'. Scientists are allowed, indeed expected, to be inquisitive about events that are not unexpected. What makes the man in the street want explanations is surprise, but in the case of the scientist it is the self-induced, artificial and chronic surprise which we call 'curiosity'; and his curiosity leads him, as I shall suggest shortly, to ask a special kind of question.

THE INSTRUMENTAL NEUROSIS

Curiosity is a motive in its own right; the satisfaction of it is the attainment of an end. It is at this point, however, that sophistication interferes with commonsense. Scientists, we are told, want explanations in order to be able to predict or manipulate future events. As a descriptive statement, of course, this is obviously too sweeping. Some scientists are simply curious, and have no interest, or only a secondary interest, in the practical applications of their explanations. To be fair however, to what is sometimes called the 'instrumental'[1] view of scientific explanation, it is intended not as a mere psychological statement about scientists' motivations, but as a requirement for an acceptable explanation: it is a prescription rather than a description.

EXPLANATION AND PREDICTION

This prescription needs a very critical examination. Does the instrumental view insist that an explanation which offers no help in predicting or manipulating the future is in some way a pseudo-explanation? One can certainly concede right away that if an explanation clearly yields a prediction about the future which turns out to be false it casts considerable doubt on the *truth* of the explanation. In other words, predictive utility is a good test of an explanation. But that is not to say that it is an *essential feature* of one. Michael Scriven has demolished this point of view in a passage which is too long to quote here. He points out that many historical explanations cannot

[1] See, for example, E. J. Meehan's *Explanation in Social Science: a system paradigm*, 1968.

yield real predictions; and that some scientific explanations—
for example, of collapses of bridges—cannot really help us to
predict the next catastrophe of this kind. As he sums up his
argument

'. . . any prediction specifically associated with an explanation is (i) often conditional[2] and (ii) either so general
as to be almost empty or so specific as to refer to no other
case, and (iii) often not assertible until it is known the
event occurred, i.e. not a true prediction'. (p. 190)

EXPLANATION AND MANIPULATION

But what about the *manipulation* of the future? One does not
always have to be able to predict exactly when a disaster is going
to happen in order to be able to prevent it. Engineers use 'safety
margins' when designing the strength of bridges. Explanations
of lightning will not tell us exactly where it is going to strike,
but they will warn us to keep away, during thunderstorms,
from trees, telegraph poles, rock spires and any other protuber-
ances from the earth's surface.

We can grant unhesitatingly that some explanations help us
to prevent what we want to prevent and produce what we want
to produce; and that when they do our confidence in them is
reinforced. But to say that a genuine explanation *must* help us
to predict, prevent or produce is ridiculous. History and
astronomy provide the most obvious exceptions. The explanation of Xerxes' invasion of Europe in 481 B.C. will not help
us to predict, prevent or produce another invasion of anywhere
by anyone, not even of Greece by Persia. The explanation of the
formation of galaxies or the explosions of supernovae will not
help us to predict, prevent or produce these cosmic events.

Of course there is no reason why one should not declare

[2] i.e. subject to 'ifs' that cannot be verified in advance.

either a personal or a political preference. One can say, 'I have no scientific curiosity: I am interested only in explanations which have practical utility'. Or one can recommend, as a matter of policy, that scarce resources should not be devoted to history, astronomy or other sciences whose explanations are of negligible utility. Social scientists who want to improve societies are apt to regard the satisfaction of mere intellectual curiosity as dillettantism. This is a matter of personal or political choice; but it has nothing to do with the difference between a genuine and a pseudo-explanation.

EXPLANATION AND CULPABILITY

There is a third function of explanation which must not be overlooked, because it is peculiar to explanations of law-breaking and the infringement of moral norms. Often we want an explanation of an act or acts in order to assess the actor's culpability. Unless one takes the rare and extreme view that moral blame should not be attached to any infraction of norms or the equally extreme and even rarer view that all infraction of norms are equally blameworthy, the explanation of an infraction (assuming that it commands belief) is bound to affect the degree of blame. A motorist who runs over a pedestrian because his brakes failed through no neglect of his would be blameless in most people's eyes. Less blameless would be the motorist who had been warned that his brakes were defective, but could not be bothered to have them seen to. If he were too drunk to brake in time we should be quite censorious. If he intentionally ran the pedestrian down we would be very censorious, unless perhaps we were told that the pedestrian himself had culpably run over the motorist's child.

A determinist might try to blur these distinctions by arguing that since the laws of nature made each of these situations inevitable the motorist who deliberately ran over the pedestrian without provocation could no more 'help it' than the one whose brakes failed. It is possible, however, to believe that human actions are determined and still draw distinctions of the kind which we have in mind when we say that one man could 'help it' while another could not. Suppose the motorist who is intent on revenge sees that the scene is under the observation of a policeman, and postpones the idea until he can safely carry it out. We would have to say he was capable of refraining, whereas if he had run his enemy down regardless of the policeman we might say that he was incapable of refraining.[3]

This is only one example of many distinctions which can be drawn even by people who believe that all our actions can be explained. I do not want, however, to penetrate too far into the old labyrinth of arguments about free-will and moral judgements: simply to make two points. One is that explaining actions does not necessarily abolish the basis for moral praise or blame, but on the contrary is essential to them. The other is that to explain is not always to excuse; in some cases it may have the opposite result.

Once we have recognised, however, that explanations of human actions are sometimes put forward with this aim in mind the question arises whether explanations which have this objective must differ in any way from those which have one of the other quite distinct objectives which have been discussed —the satisfaction of scientific curiosity or the utilitarian objective of prediction, prevention, or production of events.

It is not difficult to see how instrumental explanations might sometimes differ from those of the inquisitive scientist. For example, the complete scientific explanation includes an exhaustive list of a set of sufficient conditions, each of which must be

---

[3] In a well-known Australian trial of a man who had shot another while in an abnormal mental state a medical witness was asked the very good question, 'Would he have done it with a policeman at his elbow?' (He said that he would). In a Californian case a man called Gorshen actually did shoot another man with a policeman at both elbows.

fulfilled if what is being explained to take place.[4] The instrumental explanation need identify only those amongst sufficient conditions which yield accurate predictions, or which can be manipulated so as to prevent or produce whatever it is that is feared or desired. One can predict that a car will come to a stop within 10 miles merely by looking at the petrol gauge, and prevent this merely by stopping at the next filling-station, whereas a complete scientific explanation of what kept the car in motion would be much more elaborate. This scarcely amounts to an important logical difference; I use it merely to illustrate that the aim of the explanation may in practice determine its form. As for the kinds of explanation which are involved in lawyers' assessments of culpability, these have been dissected by Hart and Honoré in *Causation in the Law* (1959). I shall argue, however, in Chapter 2 that an explanation needed for the assessment of culpability will tend to be of a particular kind.

It is the sort of explanation required by intellectual inquisitiveness, however, rather than the needs of the social reformer or moralist, which the following chapters will discuss. Nevertheless, the social reformer need not fear that they will be useless to him, for a scientist's explanation, if sound, ought to answer the reformer's question, namely 'What can I do to prevent this evil or produce that benefit?' The scientist is, as it were, the quarryman and the social reformer is the builder, to whom not all that the quarry produces is of use. Sometimes, indeed, it may produce nothing of use: the scientist's honest answer to the question, 'What can be done?' may be 'Nothing'. For reasons which will become clearer in the next chapter this is quite often in the case.

Clearly the point of view put forward in this chapter means that the criteria of a satisfactory explanation must be to some extent subjective. In the last analysis it is for the questioner to

[4] There can of course, be alternative (and overlapping) sets of sufficient conditions.

say what sort of explanation satisfies him. This troubles people who feel that there ought somehow to be a completely objective standard by which anyone could tell whether an explanation was of the 'right' kind and, if so, was satisfactory. There are of course some more or less objective criteria, mostly logical, by which an explanation can be judged *un*satisfactory by anyone capable of grasping the criterion. Examples are tautology,[5] internal inconsistency, *non sequiturs*[6] and irrelevance.

Irrelevance, however, has both an objective and a subjective aspect. If I ask 'Why is Smith getting drunk?' it cannot by any stretch of imagination be relevant to answer 'Because, unknown to him, an earthquake has just happened in Chile'. It *is* relevant to reply 'Because it's Friday', even if the questioner does not know that Friday is pay-day and that Smith's first use for his pay is to buy alcohol. But is it relevant to explain that Smith has been drinking alcohol, and that the effects of penetration of the blood-brain barrier by alcohol is what we call drunkenness? It depends on what the questioner wanted to know. He might not be scientifically curious,[7] but simply be puzzled at Smith's deciding or allowing himself to get drunk.[8] If so, however, he should be able to tell us why he regards the answer as irrelevant. In general, he must be able to state a rational ground for being dissatisfied with an explanation: that he does not know enough science, or enough about Smith or his culture, to understand the answer, or that it is not an answer to the question he was trying to ask.

[5] Is it, for example, tautologous to say 'A major cause of crime is the criminal law?' See the discussion in Chapter 4.

[6] Is it, for example, a *non sequitur* to say 'X was followed by Y because it is followed by Y in 85 per cent of instances?' See the next chapter.

[7] As the next chapter shows, scientific explanations are sometimes irrelevant in another way.

[8] This point is pursued in Chapter 11.

B

2 How many kinds of explanation?

Another neurosis of criminologists—and other social scientists—is their preoccupation with one sort of explanation: the 'scientific' sort. It is the assumption that this is the only respectable kind which has produced the recent wave of anti-positivism amongst British sociologists of deviance, some of whom[1] go so far as to assert that 'understanding' should completely replace 'explanation' (see Chapters 8 and 9). Both points of view ignore at least one type of explanation which is not only in frequent use but is logically defensible in the appropriate circumstances. Both sides, too, seem to take for granted that everyone is agreed as to what is and what is not a scientific explanation. Some of the disputants, it is true, give—or more often imply—rather naive definition of scientific explanations: for example, as explanations of regularities (ignoring the fact that we demand and are given scientifically explanations of unique events, such as the creation of the universe).[2] Less naively, scientific explanations are equated with causal explanations,[3] so that all non-causal explanations become unscientific. This is regarded as a little loose nowadays, partly because modern scientific explanations do not take the form 'X is caused by Y', partly because of difficulties in defining what causation is. I shall be suggesting in Chapter 6, however, that definitions in terms of causation show a certain amount of insight which is missing from the currently fashionable definition.

[1] e.g. Michael Phillipson, from whom I shall be quoting later.

[2] There are, of course, other demonstrations of the inadequacy of this definition. We would not regard as scientific an explanation of a regularity which simply said 'That's how God wishes it to be'.

[3] Karl Popper (1959 § 12) seems to imply that he accepts this definition.

This defines a scientific explanation as one which is expressed in terms of laws. According to Hempel (p. 247–8) for example, the criteria for an 'adequate' scientific explanation are

(i) that the *explanandum*[4] must be a logical consequence of the *explanans*[4];

(ii) the *explanans* must contain general laws, which must actually be required for the derivation of the *explanandum*;

(iii) the *explanans* must have empirical content: i.e., be capable at least in principle of test by experimentation or observation;

(iv) the sentences constituting the *explanans* must be true.

The last of these requirements is odd. Could not an explanation be said to be scientific, adequate and yet untrue? Hempel is of course anxious to avoid any taint of subjectivity: otherwise he might have said, more plausibly and precisely, that we do not *accept* an explanation which fulfils all the other requirements if we believe it to be untrue. As for the requirement that there be some testable empirical content, this is intended merely to ensure that there is some way of telling whether the explanans is true or false. Note, however, that Hempel is forced to insert 'at least in principle', for there are many explanations—especially in astronomy—whose truth is in practice untestable. Indeed, as Ryan (1970) points out, there are laws which hardly seem capable of being tested even in principle: his example is Newton's law of motion which says that a moving body which is not acted upon by any force continues in a state of uniform motion in a straight line.[5]

It is requirements (i) and (ii), however, which are not merely criteria of adequacy but the core of Hempel's definition of a scientific explanation. It must embody general[6] laws of which

---

[4] 'Explanandum' means 'that which is to be explained' (sometimes called 'explicandum': both are respectable Latin). 'Explanans' is 'that which explains'.   [5] I return to this point on page 51.

[6] By 'general' Hempel means 'applying to a class of things and not

the explanandum is a logical consequence. Again there are awkward questions to be answered. The first is raised by the term 'logical consequence'. So long as laws take a non-probabilistic form (e.g. '*All* Xs do Y') one has only to identify the explanans as a case of X to make it logically necessary that it should do Y. But suppose that we accept—as scientists are nowadays are forced to—laws of the form 'Xs almost always Y' or '90 per cent of Xs do Y': then it is logically possible that a particular X will not Y. So if it does Y, can this be said to be a logical consequence of the law? This problem has given Hempel—and others—a great deal of trouble.

None of these difficulties are conclusive objections to the covering law definition of scientific explanation. One does not *disprove* a definition, although one can sometimes *discredit* it, for example by showing that people whose usage is important do not in fact obey it. An important example will be discussed in Chapter 6 (p. 60). The purpose of this chapter is to suggest that this particular definition misses the main point; and that the point which it misses is what it is that we demand of a scientific explanation.

In *Laws and Explanations in History* (1957)—a book which has gradually come to receive some of the attention it deserves— the philosopher W. H. Dray makes a distinction of great importance. He points out that when we ask for an explanation we are only sometimes asking 'Why is or was that necessarily so?' More often what we are really asking is 'How was that possible?' He illustrates this by citing a baseball game in Victoria, British Columbia, in which a radio commentator told listeners that a long fly ball to centre field was going to strike high up on the fence (which was twenty feet in height) and yet told them in the next breath that the centre fielder had managed

merely to particular things'. He does not, unfortunately, discuss the possibility that the behaviour of an individual human being (or animal) might in certain respects be explicable only by laws which held good of that individual only: see Chapter 12.

to catch it. What his listeners wanted to know was how he could possibly have done so (the explanation was that the ball had fallen practically onto the scorer's platform, and that the fielder had had time to run up the platform's ladder). Put more strikingly, what they wanted to be told was why the catch was not impossible, and not why it was inevitable.

Dray is concerned to emphasise that most historical explanations are of this kind, designed to answer 'how-possibly' questions rather than 'why-necessarily' ones. Little notice has been taken of his distinction, at least outside the literature of the philosophy of history,[7] and the aim of this chapter is to suggest that its importance for the explanation of human behaviour, and especially misbehaviour, has been overlooked.

Dray's distinction applies, of course, not only to the explanation of human or even animal behaviour, but also to the explanation of occurrences in the inanimate world. Faced with the collapse of a bridge. the malfunctioning of a car or the occurrence of a tidal wave we want to know how these could have happened, not why they were inevitable. Notice that it is the unexpected event for which we are prepared to accept such explanations. Where we regard the event as a regular occurrence we want to know why it is regular, or as Dray would say why it necessarily occurs.

A number of points have to be made before we consider the application of this distinction to human behaviour. First, it is obviously a valid distinction *whether or not it is used to define scientific explanations*. It is perfectly rational to cling to the covering law definition of scientific explanation and yet recognise the importance of the difference between necessity- and possibility-explanations. It is the circumstances in which we demand possibility- or likelihood-explanations that tend to differ in kind, as we shall see shortly.

Second, it is a pity that Dray drew a hard and fast line by

[7] Daniel Taylor (pp. 86ff.) devotes a few pages to it, but again in the context of historical explanation.

talking about necessity. Nowadays we are prepared, even when faced with regularities in events, to accept explanations which show that the events in question are likely to occur rather than bound to. My version of Dray's point would in effect distinguish possibility-explanations from *likelihood-* ones.

It may be objected that this turns his distinction into one of degree rather than kind. But is this an objection? After all, when we ask 'Why . . . ?' we may expect only a possibility-explanation yet get a necessity- or likelihood- one, without feeling that it is in any way an inappropriate answer.

Fourth, possibility-explanations do not discard laws of the kind that figure in necessity- or likelihood-explanations.[8] If we ask how an iceberg could appear as far south as Rockall, we may be told a story involving a particularly hard winter in Greenland, the prevailing currents in the North Atlantic, strong north-westerly winds in the spring, and a particular relationship between the shapes of the underwater and abovewater parts of the iceberg which made it 'tack' south-east under the force of these winds. This story will not deny any of the laws of meteorology, oceanography or dynamics; on the contrary, it satisfies us by showing how the iceberg's position was possible without falsifying any of these laws. Indeed, at certain points—for example, the way in which icebergs sometimes tack—the questioner may need to have the dynamics of keels and sails explained to him: but that will depend on his knowledge. The main point is that possibility-explanations do not contradict relevant likelihood-explanations.

What they often do, of course, is to involve—by implication as least—likelihood-explanations of more than one kind. The explanation of how an iceberg came to be seen off Rockall involves explanations drawn from oceanography, meteorology and physics. Possibility-explanations tend to be narratives, in

---

[8] Unless it is essential to distinguish the two kinds, I shall from now on use 'likelihood-explanation' to include 'necessity-explanation'.

which each sequence of events may be explicable in terms of quite different laws, so that if the questioner demanded it a likelihood-explanation could be provided for each. It is conceivable that a possibility-explanation might consist of a single pair of events, or at least that the only interesting part of it consisted of a single pair, and that the sequence was explicable entirely in terms of, say, the laws of thermodynamics. But this would not be typical.

Fourth, it is not only likelihood-explanations that must satisfy Popper's (1959: IV) requirement that they be empirically falsifiable. A possibility-explanation too should be of such a form that we can put to the test the question whether any of the sequences of events which it alleges could have occurred: for example, whether a baseball fielder could have run up a twenty-foot ladder in time to catch a falling ball.

Fifth, possibility-explanations are as applicable to human (or animal) behaviour as to events in inanimate nature. Indeed, when Dray originally drew his distinction it was in order to clarify the nature of many historical explanations of the actions of people. As he points out, historians often want to know why people behaved in a way that seems unlikely, and they are satisfied by an account which makes it clear how they *could* have acted as they did, without demanding what would in most cases be impossible—an account which showed that what they did was inevitable. In other words, the 'possibility' in possibility-explanations includes psychological as well as physical possibility. I make this point because some people believe that these are two quite different kinds of possibility, and I do not want to appear to ignore this belief. The point will crop up again in Chapter 9.

Thus possibility-explanations are especially in demand for *unexpected* events and actions. They are less often acceptable in the case of events which are seen as regular and therefore expected. We do not want to know how the sun could possibly have risen at 6.00 a.m. this morning: we want to know why this was inevitable. But if one clear day it does not rise at the usual time we might be satisfied with a possibility-explanation in terms of an eclipse, a change to Summer Time or an air flight to a later time-zone. Similarly, if we observe that people regularly shake hands on being introduced we do not want to know why A could possibly have shaken hands on being introduced to B, although we may want to know how the custom of hand-shaking became so prevalent in Western cultures that he was highly likely to do this.

This point is of great importance for would-be explainers of what I have called misbehaviour. A good deal of misbehaviour is unexpected behaviour. This is not to be misunderstood as a definition of misbehaviour: I shall be discussing in Chapter 10 what sort of definition might be acceptable. I am not even saying that all or even most instances of unexpected behaviour are misbehaviour: merely that a lot of misbehaviour is unexpected. Behaviour may be unexpected because it is not what in our experience most people do, or not what the person in question does, or contrary to a law, a convention or a visible notice, or has consequences which are obviously very dangerous or painful.

On the other hand, misbehaviour may be seen as regular;[9] that is, as regularly occurring behaviour. The first time a person is caught stealing we may want to know how this was psychologically possible for him: the second or third time we begin to wonder whether there is something about him or his situation that makes him likely to steal. The same is true of a person's breaches of good manners, or of his professional code. As soon as we begin to see them as part of a regularity we want a likelihood-explanation. The regularity, of course, need not be a regularity in the conduct of an individual. We may observe that vandalism, illegal parking or jostling for places on public

---

[9] Perhaps I should make it clear to the etymologically minded ethnomethodologist that I am not here using 'regular' in its archaic or ecclesiastical sense, in which it means 'in accordance with a rule'.

transport are frequent in certain urban areas, or amongst certain categories of people, although we have not seen any single individual engage in it more than once. The difference between these two kinds of regularity is not important for the present argument, but will be discussed in Chapter 12.

There are thus situations in which we begin by being satisfied with possibility-explanations, but eventually come to feel the need of likelihood ones. If someone whom we have known for some time but have never seen acting violently suddenly strikes a man in the course of a conversation at a party we shall probably be satisfied if he later tells us that the other man was his wife's ex-husband and had set out to provoke him. But suppose that he is involved in a second fracas at another party, and explains that in this case the man he struck had make a joke about his wife's relations with her ex-husband. We might begin to wonder whether he was not a little over-sensitive on the subject. And a third incident of this kind would make us ask for a psychological explanation of the regularity with which he became provoked.

On the other hand, it must not be assumed that every incident for which we accept a possibility-explanation is one for which, if we knew more, we should want a likelihood explanation. The explanandum may not itself be an instance of any sort of regularity, but merely the result of a sequence of miscellaneous everyday regularities. We recognise this in the case of what we call 'accidents'. A car-driver may be blinded for a second by a flash of of sunlight or a map unfolded by his passenger, and may fail to see a pedestrian who stepped into the road without looking because he happened to be arguing fiercely with his companion. But most misbehaviour is intentional, so that we fail to recognise the accidental aspect of many of the intentional instances. A normally law-abiding driver may feel forced to park illegally or ignore traffic lights because he has overslept and is late for an important appointment. A peaceful man may be provoked into violence by a coincidence in which a man whom he finds irritating happens unwittingly to use a form of words that has a specially insulting significance for him—as, for instance, a man who has received psychiatric treatment may resent the words 'you're crazy', however lightly used. We can be made to see how a man can act 'completely out of character' by a possibility-explanation which implies no regularity apart from a miscellany of everyday physical and psychological regularities which now and again combine to produce such an incident, but which cannot and should not persuade us that it is likely.

The distinction between possibility- and probability-explanations is relevant when culpability is being assessed. We are much more inclined to excuse an action if shown it was inevitable or highly probable than if merely persuaded that it was psychologically possible. Indeed, it is tempting to say that while probability-explanations can on occasion excuse an action completely a possibility- one can at most mitigate culpability. There would be obvious exceptions. It has already been pointed out that a possibility-explanation can involve sequences of events which are seen as inevitable or highly probable; so that it could completely excuse by describing a sequence which was such that at the crucial point the accused had no choice; for example, in which a man was driving a car whose brakes happened to fail just as he approached traffic lights, or in which he sneezed uncontrollably and so swerved into a pedestrian. In such a case it would in philosopher's language be saying that the accused could not be blamed for his action because there was no action in the strict sense; that is, no intentional act or omission.

If this chapter has succeeded in demonstrating the importance of Dray's distinction—or, to be more precise, my elaboration of his distinction—for the explanation of behaviour and especially unexpected behaviour, it will have made its main point. Whether it succeeds in substituting the definition of scientific explanation as necessity- or likelihood-explanation for the fashionable definition in terms of relevant laws is another matter. One may accept the distinction while rejecting the new definition, although in that case one must be prepared to meet the argument that laws figure not only in likelihood-explanation but also in possibility-explanations, if only implicitly. Without trying to beg this question, I shall in the rest of this book use the term 'scientific' to refer to necessity- and likelihood-explanations (and Dray's term 'narrative' to refer occasionally to possibility-explanations). Nor am I under-rating the importance of scientific laws, to which two later chapters (5 and 6) are devoted.

3 Reasons in explanations

Both possibility- and likelihood-explanations can be offered for events which do and events which do not involve the behaviour of human beings or animals. There is a kind of explanation however which can figure in either possibility- or likelihood-explanations but which is confined to human or animal behaviour. We can for the moment call this kind 'reasons', although it must very soon be subdivided.

For the moment, the distinction that is being drawn between explanations which could conceivably apply to any sort of body, animate or inanimate, and those which—at least on a modern view of nature—could not. Any kind of body, whether it is a person, a cat or a car, can move because it is pushed; but only an animate body can move because it wants to. Animate bodies also behave in machine-like ways, when reflexes are stimulated or when they have epileptic fits; and a fit or a reflex is not what we should call a 'reason'.

What sort of reasons are there? We seem to distinguish three kinds.

EMOTIONS, FEELINGS

One group can be called 'emotions' or 'feelings'. We do some things because we consciously want to. We feel and act on desires for money, food, drink, sexual activity, play; on fears of animals, traffic, ghosts; on dislikes of bores, pundits, prigs, demagogues. These feelings—and of course there are other kinds—must be distinguished from 'needs'. I may need more liquid inside me without feeling thirsty, although of course at other times I may both need it and feel thirsty. Some needs—say for vitamins—have no counterpart in feeling: the only signs of them are 'symptoms'. In another sense I may be told that I need a drink, meaning that I shall be more cheerful or more amusing when I have had one; but again that does not mean that I feel the desire for one.

AIMS

We also use 'aims' in explanations, meaning by this term desires which cannot be satisfied by immediate actions. If I desire a drink, but do not have anything drinkable to hand, I may look for a place that sells drinks; if so, my aim is to drink.

RULES

Again, I may explain what I am doing by reference to some rule. I may say 'I am drinking because his health has been proposed'—that is, following the rule that when a man's health is proposed everyone present raises his glass a little too high for drinking, then lowers it to a convenient level and drinks from it (even if there is nothing worth drinking left in it).

Until recently such explanations were not thought to be of much importance, at least outside anthropology. Anthropologists were interested in the rules which answered questions such as 'Who can marry whom amongst the Ifugao?'. In 1967, however, Garfinkel suggested[1] that large areas of human conduct were in fact governed by rules, or more precisely conventions,

[1] In *'Studies in Ethnomethodology'* (1967), Prentice-Hall, New Jersey. He acknowledges his debt to Alfred Schutz, and Goffman (1963) made much the same point: but the technique is Garfinkel's. The theory has been elaborated by Romano Harré and Paul Secord in *The Explanation of Social Behaviour* (1972).

which were never or hardly ever made explicit, and which indeed were usually demonstrable only by a special technique.
This special technique consists of deliberately violating the conventions in question, or acting according to the conventions
applicable to a somewhat different social situation. If the other
participants in the situation react with surprise or resentment,
this demonstrates that one has in fact identified a convention-
governed area of behaviour. Thus in one experiment Garfinkel
persuaded 40 students to 'spend from fifteen minutes to an
hour in their homes imagining that they were boarders and
acting out this assumption. They were to conduct themselves
in a circumspect and polite fashion . . . to avoid getting personal, to use formal address, to speak only when spoken to'.
With a few exceptions, their families were 'stupefied', and
angrily or anxiously asked 'What's the matter? What's gotten
into you? Did you get fired? Are you sick? What are you being
so superior about? Why are you mad? . . .'

Since the explanation of misbehaviour is concerned to a considerable extent with rule-infringement rather than rule-ob-
servance, it may seem unlikely that rule expositions will figure
in it; but that is not so. Many infringements of one rule can be
satisfactorily explained by the information that the rule-breaker
was in fact observing another rule. In jurisdictions where it is a
crime to conceal one's knowledge that another person has committed a crime, doctors—especially psychiatrists—frequently
do this in obedience to their ethical code. Teenagers invent
games based on law-breaking. Some years ago a group of the
older boys in a British public school invented an elaborate
shoplifting competition, in which the rule was that each had to
acquire by shoplifting a complete set of a nineteenth-century
novelist's works in the same edition. Again, criminal violence is
regarded in some male groups as the obligatory response to an
insult or the invasion of their territory.

Thus a reason for an action may be that it is an immediate
response to a feeling, or is done with an aim in mind, or is a

conscious compliance with a rule. It may be more than one of these: a man with an aim in mind may select one of several actions which would achieve it because the selected action accords better with a rule, whether of law or convention, or with his preference.

But how conscious must I be of the feeling, aim or rule before it is correct to call it my 'reason' for my action? Answers to this question vary. Few if any people would insist that I must have said to myself (aloud or mentally) at the time 'I want that' or 'I shall have to do this to get that' or 'It is conventional to act thus'. It is only rarely that we act so self-consciously. Yet if reasons are to be regarded as states of mind that take place, how do we know whether they have taken place or not? Sometimes we are asked—or ask ourselves—why we did something, and are able to say, without feeling dishonest, that we did it because we felt a desire, had an aim or were observing a rule. Unfortunately there are occasions when we feel that this was not really so, and that we merely acted *as if* we were obeying a desire or a rule or had an objective in mind. In some situations our behaviour is what we call 'habitual'. This is especially likely with rule-following, which may quickly become so automatic that we may even have difficulty in recalling our adoption of the rule. As Winch points out (1958), it is not hard to tell when behaviour ceases to be rule-following and becomes habitual: it is when it ceases to be adapted to the circumstances. To say that we are following a rule in such cases is true only in a historical sense. The same can be said of many occasions on which we perform actions which were originally responses to desire: the ritual drink, the regular marital kiss are every-day examples. Actions which were originally performed with a conscious aim in mind often become habitual, whether or not they are still likely to achieve their original aim. Habitual behaviour must also be distinguished from 'automatic' behaviour such as sneezing, vomiting or having a fit. Most, if not all, habitual behaviour was originally motivated or rule-following, and more or less voluntary: one can usually refrain from it if one decides to, whereas it is impossible, or very difficult, to refrain from, or set in motion, automatic behaviour.

As we shall see in Chapter 9 there is a controversy over the question whether reasons can be causes, the assumption being that if the answer is 'yes' they can figure in 'scientific' explanations, but otherwise not. For the moment, however, it seems significant to note that whether the explanation is of a likelihood or merely of a possibility there is no *prima facie* objection to include in it such concepts as motives, aims, and rules (unless of course one is talking about inanimate objects). Certainly in everyday discourse we use them to convince ourselves or other people that what someone did was either likely or at least not psychologically impossible.

4 Unsatisfactory kinds of explanation

Meanwhile, however, there are some kinds of explanation which *can* be dismissed as unsatisfactory.

FINAL CAUSES

The first of these is a legacy from Aristotle, who distinguished four kinds of cause: material, efficient, final and formal. In his well-known example, the making of a statue, the material cause is the stone from which it is sculpted, the efficient cause is the sculpting, and the final cause is what the sculptor is aiming at —the finished statue. (The formal cause is discussed later in this chapter). Since most of Aristotle's examples are things which people make or do it was possible for him to talk in this way without drawing a distinction between the result of what they do and what they have in mind to achieve when they do it. Thus 'health' is the final cause of going for a walk. But he extended the notion to processes in which intentions are not involved, such as the way in which plants grow leaves in order (as he thought) to protect their fruit.

The notion of final causes and its mediaeval development in Thomist philosophy would be of no more than historical interest if it were not for its apparent revival in the sociological kind of explanation called 'functionalism'. According to functionalists societies have features such as laws, and even law-breaking, *because these have good consequences for the societies which have them.* Laws minimise conflict between members of a society. Law-breaking, thought Durkheim, is sometimes the

C

initiation of a needed reform without which the society would suffer. Criminal rackets, thought Merton, enable people to satisfy needs which either nobody in the society can satisfy or which only privileged people can satisfy legally.[1]

The notion that such features of a society exist because of their good consequences for that society can be interpreted in several ways:

a. HISTORICAL. What might conceivably be meant is simply that laws were originally introduced by people who foresaw their good consequences. This process can certainly be observed when particular laws are passed; but historians and anthropologists are not in a position to describe the introduction of the first law in a natural society whose members were hitherto without the concept of law. It may be partly for this reason that sociologists hesitate to adopt this interpretation of functionalism. But another reason is that some, following Merton (op. cit.), believe in *latent* functions; that is, beneficial consequences of which nobody is aware until the sociologist points them out. Merton's example of criminal rackets has already been cited, although in that case it is legitimate to ask 'Just how latent is the function, if the racketeers and the people who resort to them know why they exist?'

b. DARWINIAN.[2] On the other hand what may be meant is that in whatever way laws were first introduced it is only societies which have laws that survive. Thus laws might be imposed by conquerors on a small society to which the

---

[1] (1949, Chapter III). He does not say explicitly what would happen to the society if these needs of the underprivileged were not satisfied.

[2] Strictly speaking Aristotle's predecessor Empedocles and not his successor Darwin is entitled to the credit for propounding the notion of natural selection. If Aristotle had not discredited it with his arguments about final causes the notion might not have had to be rediscovered, and science might not have been led up a blind alley, as Bertrand Russell put it, for 2,000 years.

institution was unfamiliar, not because the conquerors had the welfare of that society in mind, but simply because its members would otherwise give trouble; yet the imposition of law might conduce to the survival of that society in a later era.

c. CYBERNETIC. Again what may be meant is that a society is constructed like a goal-seeking machine, such as a thermostatically controlled central heating system, for which the goal is the maintenance of the house temperature between narrow limits. The institutions of law is then regarded as a device for ensuring that something, which might be conflict, does not escalate to a disastrous level. This interpretation is not quite complete, since it begs the question 'How was such a system created?' to which the answer might be either historical (i.e. 'So-and-so did, with this deliberate aim') or Darwinian (i.e. 'It happened for other reasons, but had this survival value').

d. ARISTOTELIAN/THOMIST. On the interpretation which Aristotle probably and Thomas Aquinas certainly would have endorsed, the beneficial consequences are a necessary condition of law in a society. This does not mean merely that if there were no beneficial consequences nobody could have created the institution with them in mind. That would be an historical interpretation, and history is full of people who foresaw beneficial consequences of their creations but were wrong. It means that the beneficial consequences themselves are a necessary condition even if people are incapable of foreseeing them. What is out of the ordinary about this interpretation is that it applies the concept of necessary condition to *future* events, and not to contemporary or past events as is usual. It thus has two implications, also eccentric. One is that the direction of causation in time must be two-way; for the institution of law must both cause and be caused by these later events. The other is that something can be a necessary condition even if it never happens; for after all the society may be destroyed by war or natural disaster before the beneficial consequences can eventuate.

To sum up, the only interpretation of functional explanations which makes them *logically* distinguishable from other kinds is in terms of final causes, a notion which contradicts modern assumptions about the nature of causation and its direction in time.

FORMAL CAUSES

A more recent Aristotelian revival is the notion of formal cause. 'By definition, a major cause of crime is the criminal law itself' said Dr. Stan Cohen in a broadcast talk (1973). He was echoing the authors of *The New Criminology*,[3] in which the legal prohibitions of certain acts are called the 'formal cause' of crime. They had borrowed the term—with due ackowledgement— from Theodore Sarbin and Jeffrey Miller who in turn had got the idea from Edwin Lemert (1967). But whereas Lemert talks of 'original' and 'effective' causes, about which (as we shall see) he has a perfectly valid point to make, the substitution of the Aristotelian term 'formal cause' and the use of the phrase 'by definition' has confused the issue by plunging us into scholastic metaphysics.

We have seen what Aristotle meant by material, efficient and final causes. The notion of *formal* causes needs a little more explanation. It is the essence of a statue that it is a representation of something: this is what makes it a statue instead of a mere piece of irregularly shaped stone. If it were not a representation it would not be a statue: being a representation is its formal cause. In the same way, Cohen and the authors of *The New Criminology* would argue, a crime is by definition conduct

[3] Ian Taylor, Paul Walton and Jock Young (1973: 46, 65).

which is prohibited by the criminal law: unless it were prohibited it would not be a crime. Similarly, to be deviant an
action must be regarded as such. So the criminal law or the
disapproval of others are the formal causes of crimes or
deviance, as the case may be.

At first sight there is little wrong with talking in this
mediaeval way. If one wants to emphasise that a necessary condition of an action's being a crime is that it should fulfil the
definition of a crime—that is, be prohibited by the criminal law
in the jurisdiction within which it takes place, and if one feels
that this tautology is made more impressive by using the
language of Aristotle and Aquinas, is any harm done?

But it is more serious if the aim of doing so is to imply without actually saying so that we should not have the misbehaviour
in question—or at least not so much of it—if we had not been
so ill-advised as to prohibit it. The logical fallacy is obvious.
Granted that breaking into other people's premises without
their permission would not be a crime if it had not been prohibited by criminal law, that does not entail that people would
not do it, or would do it less often. Commonsense might even
suggest that more people would do it, and the same people
would do it more often.

On the other hand, there are some valid points which Cohen
and his colleagues sometimes link with this fallacy. First, there
is John Stuart Mill's point that we use, or try to use, the criminal
law to discourage quite a number of sorts of behaviour which
ought not to be penalised because they harm only the doer.
Mill's point was a moral one; but latter-day utilitarians have
added the more forceful argument that there are also types of
criminal behaviour of which the harm may be imaginary, or
which, though undeniably harmful, are not really influenced
by the criminal law. To point this out, however, is not to
answer the question 'Why do people behave in these ways?'.
Instead it suggests the entirely separate question 'Why do
societies (i) disapprove so much of these forms of behaviour and

(ii) resort to the criminal law rather than other ways of dis-
couaraging them?'.

Secondly, there is Lemert's point about 'secondary deviance':
that some people break the law because they have been labelled
as law-breakers. The mechanism underlying this generalisation
may be the simple reluctance of employers to give legitimite
employment to people with criminal records, so that the latter
see illegitimate acquisition as their only opportunity. Sometimes
ostracism compels the convicted person to seek companionship
amongst people ostracised for similar reasons, so that he becomes a member of a group whose rules of conduct permit or
even encourage law-breaking. Sometimes the labelling process
changes his own view of himself, so that he believes himself to
be the sort of person who is bound to behave as the label says
he does. To tell someone that he is an alcoholic may well
destroy any confidence he had in his ability to control his drinking. These and other mechanisms have been suggested and
described by 'labelling theorists'.[4] It is fair to say that they have
been credibly described rather than demonstrated, and it is
worth noting that although two social psychologists—Freedman
and Doob—have carried out experiments which give limited
support to labelling theory, their book is not cited by the sociologists who are most in need of such evidence. In any case
labelling theorists are not trying to answer either the question
'Why has this or that society resorted to making this or that
form of conduct criminal?' or the question 'Why do people
indulge in it at all?' but the question 'Why are people who have
indulged in it likely to go on doing so?'.[5]

There is yet another question, however, which it is sensible

[4] In particular by one of the authors of *The New Criminology:* see
Jock Young's illuminating essay (1971).

[5] The bigoted labelling theorist seems to believe that his is the only
answer to the question: the broad-minded one admits that people sometimes repeat their misbehaviour because they enjoy it, or get into the
same sort of situations, or for other obvious reasons. But that is a side-
issue.

to ask. Given that a certain kind of behaviour is an infringement of the criminal law, given that some people nevertheless
infringe the law in this way, and given that their behaviour is
observed by others whose values are law-abiding, why are some
of the infringements seen as such, others not? Why is a fight
between football players seen as a matter for the referee rather
than the police, when there is no law that excuses assaults on
the football field? Again, a man who offers a tentative sexual
caress to a woman who knows him will at worst have it rejected; but if he is a stranger the same gesture may lead to his
being charged with indecent assault. There are subtler deter-
minants than these, of course: the conventions governing the
perception of thefts as thefts or as mere taking of perquisites are
complex and vary from organisation to organisation. (Some
organisations tacitly allow employees of certain ranks to claim
first-class travelling expenses even if they choose to travel sec-
ond-class: others treat this as fraud.) There is a profitable field
of study here which has been barely entered; but my object is
simply to demonstrate that those who do enter it are trying to
answer a *third* sort of question.

Fourthly, it is undoubtedly the case that *some* infringements
of the law would not be committed if they were not infringements of the law. Adolescents and even older people will steal
because of the excitement which they get out of risking arrest.
Others break the law as a protest, either against the irration-
ality—real or supposed—of the prohibition itself, or against the
legitimacy of the prohibiting authority. If one believes that the
King of England has no right to tax one's tea one may empty
it into Boston harbour. If one believes that it is irrational to prohibit the use of cannabis while countenancing the use of nico-
tine, alcohol and tranquilisers, one may smoke it as a protest.
These situations come nearer than any other to justifying the
assertion that 'if it weren't a crime they wouldn't do it'. But
they are of course rather special situations, and are far from
being what is meant by the authors of *The New Criminology*.

It is possible that they are really trying to make a fifth point:
that crime is so serious a problem because there are a lot of
things which people will inevitably do, but which societies—or
the power-wielding élites in societies—are ill-advised enough to
discourage by means of the criminal law. I am tempted to nick-
name this 'Eden-ideology' because one of the implications of
the third chapter of Genesis is that Adam and Eve were happy
and harmless nudists until they were 'criminalised' by the
knowledge of good and evil and the punishment of Jehovah.

Eden-ideology is again based on something that happens
occasionally but not nearly often enough to be made the basis
of an ideology. There are situations in which people are happily
and harmlessly doing something when they are suddenly told
that it is wicked or illegal. The missionaries' imposition of clothes
on South Sea islanders was a latter-day enactment of Adam and
Eve's criminalisation. In present-day Britain the Ministry of
Transport has decided that for their own good people must be
discouraged by the criminal law from riding motor-cycles without crash-helmets. But Eden-ideology is quite inapplicable to
crimes such as murder, rape, robbery or burglary, which have
been serious crimes in every civilised culture—and most uncivil-
ised ones too—for many generations. If asked why a young man
illegally rides his motor-cycle without a crash-helmet one may
reasonably explain that he was in the habit of doing so before
it was made a crime, and either forgot the new law or felt that
nobody had the right to force him to wear a helmet. But this
sort of answer will not satisfy anyone in his senses where long-
established crimes are concerned. In this case the question must
be 'Why, in a society in which such actions have for generations
been treated as criminal and are severely punishable, are they
committed?'

To call the criminal law 'formal cause' of crime, however,
is an intellectual sleight of hand by which the answers to other
questions are palmed off on us as if they were the answer to
this question. Those other questions are also intellectually

fascinating, but this fascination is apt to conceal the fact that they are completely distinct. The purpose of this sleight of hand is also perfectly respectable: to emphasise the part which 'society'—to use that loose but popular phrase—plays in generating criminal behaviour. But there are more straightforward and convincing ways of doing so which do not need to be dressed up in scholastic jargon.

CLASSIFICATORY EXPLANATIONS

Another unsatisfactory kind of explanation is what Daniel Taylor calls a 'what-explanation'. Sometimes, he points out, we are satisfied by an answer to a why-question which simply tells us to what class of events the thing that puzzles us belongs. 'Why are those young people milling around in the square?' Answer: 'It is a demonstration'; or—a more precise classification—'It is a demonstration against examinations'. Again, events not involving human beings or animals may be similarly explained. If we ask why the house is rocking we may be told 'It's an earthquake'.

There is no doubt that we do answer why-questions in this way, and that the answers are often completely satisfactory to the questioner. But are the answers logically distinct from the three types of explanation that have been described? Certainly it is impossible to think of a 'what-explanation' which could not be expanded into an explanation of one of those kinds, without the slightest inconsistency. And the fact that the questioner may be satisfied with the answer 'It's an earthquake' does not mean that the explanation is not scientific: only that he knows enough science to be satisfied with this concise reply. Of course, if he believes that earthquakes are messages from an angry god telling him to stop whatever he is doing, the answer will for him be a short-hand form of a reason-explanation; and this may or may not be what the answerer meant. This possibility of ambiguity is another reason for being suspicious of classificatory explanations.[6]

This is not to deny that classificatory explanations have their uses. If I ask 'Why did he try to kill himself?' and am told in a fashionable phrase 'It was a cry for help', this guides me towards an explanation by classifying his action as a message. If I accept the classification I ask for a reason-explanation ('What sort of help did he want?'), and perhaps after that for a possibility-explanation ('How could he have got into that situation?'). All that I am arguing is that an explanation by classification is neither *sui generis* nor complete.

[6] Taylor recognises the closeness of the relationship between what-explanations and motivational ones, but concludes surprisingly that the latter are a sub-division of the former! (Ch. V).

5 What does a scientific explanation consist of?

Let me sum up the argument so far. It is naive to assume that the only aim of explanation is the prediction or manipulation of phenomena: the satisfaction of curiosity and the assessment of culpability are equally legitimate aims. It is also naive to assume that the only completely acceptable sort of explanation is scientific. It is true that there are several sorts of pseudo-explanations: in terms of final causes, formal causes or classifications. But there is at least one kind of genuine explanation which is logically quite distinct from the scientific: the narrative kind. There are also explanations in terms of reasons, which *may* be of a third sort. There is no incompatibility between the genuine kinds of explanation. For example, one may sensibly ask for a scientific explanation of the following of one event by another in a narrative explanation; and I shall be arguing (in Chapters 8 and 9) that explanations in terms of reasons may figure in scientific or narrative explanations.

Meanwhile, however, it is necessary to say a good deal more about scientific explanations. If, as has been suggested, they are answers to the question 'Why would it have been surprising if that had not happened?', what sort of statements are satisfying answers to such statements?

SATISFACTORY SCIENTIFIC EXPLANATIONS

The first point to be made is that they must satisfy not only a certain logical requirement but also the individual questioner. The logical requirement is that the answer must at the least convey information that is not presupposed by the question: it must tell us more than we must have known in order to ask what we did. It may seem unnecessary to point this out: but social scientists are sometimes accused of offering what Professor Homans calls 'explanation by concept':

> ' . . . An anthropologist friend once said to me, in pointing out the usefulness of this concept: 'If someone asks me, for instance, why the Chinese do not like milk, I can only say 'Because of the culture'.' All I could say in return was that, if that was *all* he could say, he was not saying much. All that the use of the word 'culture' implied was that disliking milk had been characteristic of the behaviour of some Chinese for some generations. But we know that already; 'culture' did not add anything. . . . More generally, 'explanation by concept' is not explanation.' (1967, p. 12)

Homans is being a little unfair. After all, the anthropologist was in effect giving negative information of some value: that the Chinese dislike of milk was not due to any physiological peculiarity, such as difficulty in digesting milk, nor to any scientific beliefs—for example that milk carries a form of dysentery.

Nevertheless, the point is worth making; and there are examples of explanation by concept in criminology. David Matza (1964: 24) offers two instances. One is the Glueck's hypothesis that recidivists' propensity for crime eventually 'burns out'. Matza says that 'a notion like "burning out" merely reiterates the occurrence of maturational reform. It hardly explains it'. This is not completely fair to the Gluecks, who were trying to explain the supposed fact that most criminal careers seemed to last roughly the same number of years. It must be admitted, however, that the notion of burning out, though it is an attempt at an illuminating analogy of the kind discussed later in

Chapter 6, is not illuminating at all, since there is no other similarity between criminality and fire.[1] Matza's other example, the notion of adolescent maladjustment, is a better one. As he says, it 'purports to be a diagnostic category' but is 'for the most part a reiteration of the juveniles' delinquency'. Again the term 'maladjustment' is an implied analogy: but is so vague as to be quite unilluminating.

What has to be satisfied, however, is not only the logical requirement which has just been discussed, but also the individual questioner; and whether the explanation satisfies him or not depends on what he knows already and how inquisitive he is. Thus if he says 'Why did the light flicker?' he may be satisfied with the answer 'Because of the thunderstorm', or he may not, depending on his knowledge of electricity. If he does not know much, he may have to be told why thunderstorms are associated with temporary local variations in the voltage of power lines. All one can say is that the explanation must fill the gaps in the questioner's knowledge and not provoke further requests for an explanation.

INCOMPLETENESS

Thus in practice most explanations are *incomplete* from the logical point of view, even when scientists would regard them as satisfactory. They are incomplete because they take for granted—and rightly—that the people to whom they are being offered

a. know the rough meaning (if not the scientific definition) of the terms used (such as 'thunderstorms', 'voltage', 'power lines');

[1] It must also be admitted that they arrived at their supposed fact by an extraordinary misuse of statistics. See my *Crime and Punishment in Britain*.

b. know what most people know about the everyday behaviour of things (or human beings)—for example, that certain kinds of lamps work on electricity;
c. share the explainer's assumption that there is nothing abnormal about the situations to which the explanation is intended to apply (e.g., that the electric lighting is supplied as usual from a main power source with overhead lines, and not from a private source in the house).

THE IDEAL EXPLANATION

Althought really complete explanations must be rather rare, this need not prevent us from discussing what the ideal form of a scientific explanation is like. First, it defines its *explanandum*, that is, what it is intended to explain. This may be of two kinds—a particular event or state of affairs or a class of events. There is a lot more to be said, however, about *explananda*, especially the *explananda* of criminologists, and Chapters 11 and 12 are devoted to this subject.

Second, it links the explanandum to something which is commonly called 'the cause'. It is usual to say that this is an event, series of events, or state of affairs. It is probably better, as Professor Ayer points out (p. 17) to regard causal links as holding between *facts* rather than events or states, because we sometimes want to say that the cause of something was the absence of an event or state (as when we say 'his car ran down the hill while he was in the shop because he had not put on the handbrake').

The notion of 'a cause', however, raises problems. We can hardly avoid talking about 'causation', but it is desirable to avoid talking about 'a cause'. An example will show why. Suppose that we are trying to explain a forest fire. We may say either that the cause was a carelessly dropped cigarette, or that it was the abnormally dry state of the undergrowth. We tend, as Professors Hart and Honoré point out (pp. 31ff) to select some abnormal condition from among the sufficient conditions. The *sufficient*[2] conditions of a forest fire are:

a. the presence of oxygen in the atmosphere;
b. a low moisture content in much of the vegetation;
c. the application of a certain minimum degree of heat to part of the vegetation.

The presence of oxygen in the air is so normal a condition that we could scarcely call it a 'cause'. If the vegetation were usually very dry, we should not call that condition a 'cause' either, but would unhesitatingly reserve the term for the *event* consisting of the application of heat, whether by lightning or discarded cigarette. But if lightning or discarded cigarettes were common, and did not usually lead to forest fires (as in Britain), whereas the dry state of the forest was abnormal (as in Britain), we might well call that 'the cause'.

There are situations, however, in which the choice of what to call 'cause' is even more arbitrary. In the case of some traffic accidents it is difficult to decide whether to say that the cause was the high speed of the car or the sharpness of a bend in the road. Sometimes we simply select the speed of the car because it is the more 'event-like' of the two, or because not all cars travel at the speed necessary to make them skid or capsize. Sometimes we are even more illogical, and select the condition which we think we can alter (for example, by putting up a notice which will slow drivers down, or straightening the road).

It is for reasons such as these that scientists dislike the term 'cause', and regard it as fit only for colloquial use. They prefer

[2] *Sufficient* and *necessary* conditions must be distinguished. A set of sufficient conditions (they seldom come singly) make the event inevitable (subject to the reservation on p. 44 on the subject of inevitability). There may be alternative sets of sufficient conditions, which may or may not share one or more conditions. If a condition is a member of all the possible sets (i.e., if the event could never occur without it) it is a *necessary* condition.

to say that the maximum speed at which a car of such and such a weight could change direction as quickly as the bend required without overturning or skidding is, say 40 m.p.h., and that the car in question exceeded this.

This example, however, illustrates the fact that there can be more than one set of sufficient conditions for the same explicandum. A car might overturn when rounding a bend either because its speed exceeded the safety maximum or because at a certain point on the bend it became exposed to a very strong wind, and if so one would have to specify an alternative set of conditions which would include such variables as the area of the car's side, the angle and the force of the wind. This alternative set might or might not have variables in common with the first set, such as the car's speed.

Again, 'cause' is sometimes used to refer to a state of affairs which exists at the time of the event which is the explicandum (e.g. the sharpness of the bend), sometimes to identify an event immediately preceding the explicandum (e.g. the car's speed just before it overturned) and sometimes even an earlier event in a chain of events leading to the explicandum (e.g. the failure of the car's brakes on the downhill road before the bend).

These awkwardnesses in colloquial usage have to be accepted in certain kinds of discussion about causation: for example, when lawyers are trying to allocate responsibility for an accident.[3] But do they have to be accepted by social scientists? If they are trying to model themselves on natural scientists they will find, as I have pointed out, that the latter do not seem to talk of 'causes' when precision is called for.[4] Fortunately, even if one is compelled to talk about 'causation' in the social sciences, one need not talk about 'causes'. It is more precise to speak of

[3] See the very good discussion of common usage in Hart and Honoré's Chapter II.

[4] We shall see in Chapter 9 that there are philosophers of social science who think that it is not merely too imprecise but in fact misleading to talk about 'causes' of voluntary behaviour; but that is another story.

the set (or alternative sets) of sufficient conditions for the occurrence of the explicandum. But this is only the first stage.

GENERAL STATEMENTS

For we also need to be told why, given these conditions, the explanandum occurred. Now it is at least a partial answer to this question to tell us that given these conditions events similar to the explanandum always[5] do occur. In other words, the second stage is a *general statement* linking the class of events to which we have assigned the explicandum to classes of conditions such as those in the particular statement.

RELEVANCE

What can be said about these general statements? First, they must be *relevant*: that is, such that the explanandum can be seen to be an instance of what they are talking about. In simple cases this is obvious. If the explanandum is the overturning of a moving vehicle the general statement must at least be about the behavior of moving bodies supported on surfaces. Sometimes, however, there can be real doubt about the relevance of the general statement. When psychologists invoke general statements about the conditioned behaviour of a pigeon in a Skinner box as part of the explanation for the way in which we learn to do arithmetic, then we may question whether the latter is an instance of the sort of generalisations they are offering.

NON-ANALYTIC NATURE

Second, they must not be mere analytic statements: that is,

[5] or 'usually'; the difference will be discussed in a moment.

D

about definitions or the use of words. If I ask 'Why was that flash of light in the sky followed by a rumbling noise?' it is not a satisfactory explanation to reply 'That was an instance of a thunderstorm, for in thunderstorms flashes in the sky are followed by loud rumbles'. All that this tells me is that 'thunderstorm' is the name for such phenomena.[6] Some (though not all) what-explanations turn out to be of this kind.

EMPIRICAL NATURE

Third, they should be *empirical*[7] generalisations: that is, they should talk about associations of events or situations or qualities or quantities which can be experienced. This is not to say that their *truth* must be verifiable from experience,[8] merely that other instances of what they state must be unmistakably observable.[9]

[6] Yet many parents expect intelligent children to accept such pseudo-explanations.

[7] This does not automatically follow from the requirement that they should be non-analytic. For example, someone might try to explain the alleged phenomena of telepathy by saying 'All minds are really one in the Absolute', and it might be clear from further conversation with him that the truth of this did not follow from his definition of 'mind'. Yet though it would therefore be what logicians call a synthetic proposition it could hardly be said to be an empirical one. It *could* be a statement about an explanatory model (see pp. 54ff); but if—as seems likely—it failed to meet the requirements of such statements we should probably categorise it as a 'metaphysical' statement, although it could be what Toulmin calls a 'principle of inference', and as such part of a 'model' (see p. 52).

[8] For, as has been pointed out by innumerable philosophers since Hume, the *truth* of a general empirical statement is impossible to demonstrate merely by observing instances of it, however numerous.

[9] This requirement creates obvious, but not necessarily insuperable, difficulties for those who wish to argue that historical explanations are scientific.

SPECIFYING THE CONNECTION

Fourth, they must not merely assert some sort of connection between the explicandum and the other facts which they include:
they must specify the connection. Examples of fairly satisfactory
specification are:

a. Given conditions x, y . . . , When A happens, B follows
   (i.e. x, y . . . + A are a set of sufficient conditions for the
   occurrence of B);
b. Given conditions k, l . . . , when C happens, D[10] does not;
c. Given conditions m, n . . . , the Q-ness of O varies with the
   T-ness of W (or inversely with, or with the square of, etc.).

Examples of generalisations which are *not* specific enough
from this point of view are given by Homans (1967, pp. 14ff)
who calls them 'orienting statements'. He instances *inter alia*
Marx's statement that the organisation of the means of production determines the other features of a society:

> 'This is more than a definition and resembles a proposition
> in that it relates two phenomena to one another. But these
> phenomena—the means of production and the other
> features of a society—are not single variables. At best they
> are whole clusters of undefined variables. And the relation-
> ship between phenomena is unspecified, except that the
> main direction of causation—determination—is from the
> former to the latter. Whereas Boyle's Law says that, if
> pressure goes up, volume will assuredly go down, what
> Marx's Law says is that, if there is some, any, change in
> the means of production, there will be some unspecified
> change or changes in the other features of society . . .'

[10] D being something which would be expected, such as a person's
awakening from sleep in the morning.

Criminologists too give vent to 'orienting statements'. An example is Lacassagne's aphorism 'Societies have the criminals they deserve'.[11] Whether or not Lacassagne himself regarded this as a scientific statement, it has become an examiner's cliché, and candidates are regularly invited to discuss it as seriously as Marx's dictum. Yet like that dictum it does no more than tell us that if we are interested in the explanation of crime we should look at the societies in which it occurs. But at what features of these societies? Mannheim expands Lacassagne's aphorism into the statement that 'every society possesses the type of crime and of criminals which fit into its cultural, moral, social, religious and economic conditions' (p. 422); but this is only slightly more specific. What sort of crime, for example, 'fits into' what sort of social conditions? Like Homans, I am not saying that such remarks are valueless; merely that their value is often over-rated.

APPLICABILITY

Fifth, they must give some indication of what I call their 'applicability'. The sort of empirical generalisation for which scientists strive has universal applicability. It asserts that it is true whatever the conditions and without exception. It takes a form which can be expressed in this way:

(1) Whenever A then always B (or, the X-ness of A always varies with the Y-ness of B)
   Example: whenever heat is applied to a substance it expands.

More often, however, it takes a different form

(2) Whenever A, then B, unless C or D (or C *and* D) . . .

[11] A. Lacassagne, cit. W. Bonger in his *Introduction to Criminology* (English trans. 1936, 79-9): 'Les sociétés ont les criminelles qu'elles méritent'.

Example: whenever heat is applied to a substance it
expands unless
a. it is an inflammable substance and the heat is sufficient
to ignite it;
or b. it is at the melting point;
or c. the heat is conducted away very rapidly.

Statments of type (2) can be called 'generalisations of limited
but precise applicability'.

Statements of type (1) and (2) differ in applicability from
another sort of statement sometimes found in science:

(3) 'Whenever A then frequently (or "nearly always" or
"often" or "more often than not") B'.

This can logically be regarded as a statement whose applicability is subject to unspecified exceptions, and is therefore, in
my phraseology 'limited and *im*precise', although a commoner
term in the philosophy of science is 'probabilistic'.

For the moment, let us take a closer look at generalisations of
less than complete applicability, which abound in the social
sciences, and are often used by sceptics in attacks on them.
These sceptics overlook the fact that even in the sciences which
they are taking as their paragons unlimited applicability is
usually found only in statements with a negligible empirical
content. Whenever a statement has a substantial empirical content (as has the generalisation that the darker the colour of the
surface the hotter it becomes when exposed to light) it is possible
to devise exceptions to it[12] (for example, by selecting dark
materials of high conductivity and light materials of low conductivity). It is commonly said that water draining through a
hole swirls clockwise in the northern hemisphere and anti-

---

[12] The only *prima facie* exception to *this* generalisation is astronomy.
Even in this science, however, the universality of generalisations with a
high empirical content is not absolutely complete. 'Black holes' are
said to be exceptions to several otherwise universal laws.

clockwise in the southern hemisphere: but see the extract below from the Daily Telegraph.

BACK TO SQUARE ONE

The pitfalls encountered in solving other people's problems are encouragingly illustrated in 'Answering Any Questions' out from David and Charles tomorrow, a guide to setting up an information office by Margery Weiner, who founded and ran *The Daily Telegraph*'s own information Bureau for 13 years.

One example was when someone asked whether water really revolved in different directions as it ran out on different sides of the Equator. The Association of Special Libraries and Information Bureaux, the first people consulted, found that two sets of basins in their own Belgrave Square offices emptied in different directions.

Next stop was the British Hydromechanics Research Association, who said firmly that in the northern hemisphere water runs down the drain clockwise and south of the Equator anti-clockwise.

But they added the awkward rider that this was so only in theory: 'in practice perfect conditions without outside interference were needed.'

Indeed, implicit in almost all scientific generalisations with any substantial empirical content is an unspoken proviso, such as 'in the laboratory' or 'under normal conditions'. But because scientists such as chemists or physicists are usually talking about experiments carried out under laboratory conditions they do not think it necessary to be explicit about the proviso.

Nevertheless, there *is* a difference between most generalisations of the 'laboratory' sciences and most generalisations of the social sciences. Both kinds are of limited applicability, but laboratory scientists are usually able to be precise about the applicability of their generalisations, by specifying what variables must be kept constant (or within limits), whereas social scientists are often unable to do this, and have to be content with statements of the 'nearly always' sort (type (3)) or even of the 'more often than not' sort (type (4)).

It is not that social scientists fail to see the merits of precise applicability (whether of type (1) or of type (2)) but that they have difficulty in achieving this precision, and when they do it is almost always at the cost of later retraction or modification. Thus Dollard and Miller's classic study *Frustration and Aggression* began with a statement of type (1):

'Aggression is always a consequence of frustration. More specifically the proposition is that the occurrence of aggressive behaviour always presupposes the existence of frustration and, contrariwise, that the existence of frustration always leads to some form of aggression.'

As they immediately had to admit, however, 'always' needed some special pleading: there were many *prima facie* exceptions to it:

'In many adults, and even children, frustration may be followed so promptly by an apparent acceptance of the situation and readjustment thereto that one looks in vain for the relatively gross criteria ordinarily thought of as characterising agressive action. . . . This does not mean, however, that such reaction tendencies are thereby annihilated; rather it has been found that, although these reactions maybe temporarily compressed, delayed, disguised, displaced or otherwise deflected from their immediate and logical goal, they are not destroyed.'

They were thus trying to argue that these were only *apparent* exceptions. First, what might appear to be frustration of goal-directed activity was sometimes not really frustration, since the goal-seeking person or animal could often find a substitute goal: they instanced romantic fiction as a substitute for romantic experience. Secondly, in cases where frustration undeniably occurs but seems not to result in aggression, the aggression is not absent, but is 'delayed', 'disguised', 'displaced' or 'otherwise deflected'.

What they and they and their followers found more difficult to meet was the objection that there are situations in which aggression is obviously a response to other things than frustration, and in particular to attack. Their adherents had to argue that attack was a form of frustration, since it interrupted goal-seeking behaviour: but this was obviously very strained indeed. They would have done better to assert that frustration is *one* but not *the only* stimulant of aggression.

This is not too unfair an example of what makes other scientists critical of the generalisations of social scientists, which seem to be failed attempts to achieve applicability of type (1) or (2) (unlimited or limited but precise applicability). And it is true that this is what such generalisations often are. It seems to be assumed by both sorts of scientist, however, that applicability of type (3) (what I have called 'limited but imprecise') is unacceptable. Now there is no doubt that it is less satisfactory than types (1) or (2). Nor can it be denied that the form of some type (3) generalisations is unacceptable. If in Dollard and Miller's generalisation we insert the word 'often', what level of frequency are we trying to convey, and what sort of observations would confirm or, more to the point, disconfirm it?[13] But do type (3) generalisations have to be as imprecise as this?

A generalisation of this form would of course be less objectionable if instead of 'frequently' the social scientist could say 'in such-and-such a percentage of cases', or 'in a percentage of

[13] See Chapter 7 on confirmation.

cases which is not less than x nor more than y '. Such a general-isation would be sufficiently precise to be testable (what con-stitutes a test is discussed latter in Chapter 7). Even if all that he could say were 'In any animal (or group of animals) in which aggressive behaviour is sometimes observed it is observed more often when the animal (or group) has been subjected to frustra-tion than when it has not' he would be making a testable generalisation. Whether it could be regarded as a *law* or not would depend on a criterion which is discussed in the next chapter.

6 Generalisations and laws

Whatever the degree of *applicability* of an empirical generalisation—that is, whether it is of type (1), (2) or (3)—we have still to consider what gives us confidence in its *truth*. In plain terms, no matter how long a series of occasions has been observed in which F was followed by A with the frequency stated in the generalisation, it provides no logical guarantee that the generalisation will continue to be true. Only a tautology carries a guarantee of its own truth, and it does so without the need of any empirical observations.

Yet, as Alan Ryan points out (pp. 55ff and 70), we do distinguish between two sorts of generalisation: the kind which he calls 'causal laws' and those which are merely 'enumerative', or '*de facto*', in his terms. Examples of the latter are 'All European heads of states are and have been white', or 'Whenever and wherever I take a holiday it rains'. They merely state what has been found to be the case, whereas causal laws do something more: in Ryan's words they 'licence future and counterfactual statements'. If we regarded 'All European heads of states are and have been white' as a causal law, we should be implying 'are, have been and always will be white' and also implying the counterfactual statement that 'if Victoria had been black she would not have been the Queen of England'.

Obviously, then, the *meaning* of the same generalisation differs according to whether it is intended as a mere enumerative statement or as a causal law. But what is it that gives us enough confidence to offer a generalisation as a causal law? Is this confidence irrational (as Hume thought), so that the distinction between generalisations which we treat as enumerative and those we regard as causal is merely psychological? Ryan thinks not, and argues that causal generalisations are *entitled* to be distinguished. But what constitutes this entitlement?

NOTATIONS

Some people's confidence in a generalisation is increased if it can be stated in a particularly neat or impressive notation. The commonest example of this is the most concise and precise notation of all: algebra. We are extremely impressed when told that the phenomena which we call gravitational can be expressed in the form

$$G = \frac{Mmk}{D^2}$$

(G being the strength of the attraction of two bodies with masses M and m, D being the distance between them and k being Newton's constant). I am not suggesting that we should not be impressed by Newton's formula. But it is impressive because it predicts the strength of G in very different situations—for example at distances measured in inches at one extreme and thousands of miles at the other—with considerable accuracy. It is its precision that is the key to its importance rather than its conciseness. In other words, our confidence in it is increased— or should be if we are thinking clearly—not by the notation in which is expressed but merely because it is found to be very accurate whenever tested.

This simple truth is sometimes overlooked, and especially in the social sciences. Efforts are made to express generalisations about behaviour in algebraic formulae as if the mere possibility of doing so were a way of increasing our confidence in the generalisation. Perhaps it is: but if so it is a confidence trick. An example which illustrates social scientists' reverence for algebra at the expense of logic can be found in *Scientific Sociology*, by Professor David Willer:

'. . . In the absence of friction, force equals mass multiplied by acceleration. In the absence of hierarchical organisation or the formation of cliques, the number of interpersonal relationships R, in a group of N individuals is: $R = N(N-1)/2$. For an ideal gas, when P is pressure, V is volume and T is temperature, then $PV/T = $ Constant. For an ideal bureaucracy, when D is the number of tasks determined by decisions, and R the number of tasks determined by rules, then $D + R = $ Constant...' (1967: 103).

All these are cited by Willer as examples of 'scientific laws in the strictest sense'. Certainly the first and third are truly scientific generalisations that have been found more or less accurate by innumerable measurements. But they come from the 'hard' sciences. What about the examples of sociological laws? The equation dealing with interpersonal relationships is nothing more than the simple mathematical formula which tells us how many pairs can be selected from N things, or how many straight lines there can be joining a given number of points on a plane: it can be worked out *a priori* without any knowledge or observation of the real world. In other words, it is certainly not a 'scientific law in the strictest sense'. As for the other example, since it talks about 'ideal' bureaucracies and since no empirical evidence is cited for it, it is probably of the same nature. What it may be saying is that if the only way of determining tasks is by decision or by rule, then the total determined tasks must equal $D + R$; and an ideal bureaucracy is one in which the total number of determined tasks remains the same. If so, the statement is either a tautology or a mere prescription for the use of the word 'ideal' when applied to bureaucracies, but not a scientific law.

This is not an attempt to discredit *all* efforts to express generalisations about behaviour in algebraic formulae or in any other neat way. All that I am pointing out is (1) that one must take care not to be impressed by mathematical tautologies (2) that even if the formula is not a tautology its conciseness should not increase our confidence in it. Only the observation that it is more or less accurate given widely different values of all the variables should do that.

At this point we can return to Ryan's view. One of the things which, he thinks, distinguishes causal from enumerative generalisations is that the former can be tested experimentally to see whether they hold good in all conditions. And in so far as this is a psychological statement about scientists one must agree with him. Undoubtedly one of the considerations which persuades scientists to accord special status to some generalisations is the fact they that have been tested[1] under conditions designed to see whether there are exceptions to them which have not been specified in the generalisation.

Not every causal law, however, can be tested in this way. It is true that Ryan qualifies his observation by allowing that it is only 'in principle' that some causal laws can be tested experimentally; and this is no doubt meant to get over the difficulty posed by laws such as those relating to the movements of planets and their satellites, which would presumably rank as causal. But what is it that makes scientists confident that if they could test such generalisations experimentally they would not be falsified? It is not logical to answer that they are 'testable in principle', for there are generalisations which are testable in practice yet do *not* inspire this confidence: for example 'every man has his price'.

Obviously there is more to it than mere testability; and Ryan himself believes this. For he goes on to suggest that causal laws should be regarded not as mere general statement of *de facto* regularities but as 'recipes' for constructing causal histories:[2]

[1] Testing is discussed in Chapter 7.

[2] It is perhaps worth pointing out that Ryan is *not* employing Dray's concept of narrative explanation here, although he would probably say that laws were recipes for constructing such explanations also.

'Certainly no harm comes of calling them causal generalisations, for they are indeed general; their generality consists
in the fact that they offer (at best) rules for constructing an
indefinitely large number of actual and hypothetical histories. . . . It is only an account along some such lines as
this which will do justice to the traditional stumbling blocks
of empiricist philosophy of science—for example, to the
difficulty that a universal law about the behaviour of a body
moving in a right line and unaffected by any impressed
force was accepted as true, although we know that there is
certainly no case of even one such body, let alone a regular
stream of them . . .' (p. 60).[3]

This suggestion can be traced back least as far as F. P. Ramsey
who suggested in 1931 that laws of nature are not propositions
which are true or false, 'but rather set forth instructions for the
formation of such propositions...'. More recently, Stephen
Toulmin has drawn attention to a kind of generalisation in the
sciences which he called a 'principle of inference', since they
have to be assumed in order to allow explanations to be built
up. His most telling example is the assumption in geometrical
optics that light moves in straight lines (pp. 57ff). Without it
one could not explain such phenomena as refraction by drawing geometrical diagrams. It is very plausible to suggest that
Newton's Laws of Motion are of the same kind: indeed,
Newton himself called them '*axioms* or laws' (*axiomata sive
leges*). As Ryan says, there is no known instance of a body's
continuing in a state of uniform motion in a straight line because no force deflects it: yet the First Axiom of Motion is
part of the foundations of modern astronomy.

[3] The example chosen by Ryan appears at first sight to contradict the
criterion of testability which he accepts only a few pages earlier. For he
appears to be saying that the First Law of Motion is untestable, even in
principle. But he would probably argue that from it and *other laws of
motion* we can contsruct 'causal narratives' which *can* be tested.

But are Ramsey and Ryan justified in implying that *all* scientific laws are of this nature, so that one should not ask 'Are they true, or probable?' but only 'Are they applicable?'? Toulmin merely says that *some* generalisations are of this sort; and certainly there seem to be others of which it appears to make sense to ask whether they are true, and which—unlike the Axioms of Motion—seem to have observable instances. Are we wrong to talk of them as 'discoveries', and should we call them 'inspired inventions'? Take the often-cited example of Mendel's laws, dealing with the transmission of characteristics from one generation of plants or animals to another. These laws were derived from his statistics about the colour and shape of cross-bred peas. It is true that he had also to recognise the distinction between dominant and recessive characteristics, and that this recognition could well be called 'invention': but he did not invent the 3:1 ratio in which they are transmitted.[4] It is also true, however, that the way in which a generalisation is arrived at is not a conclusive argument as to its logical status: Ramsey and Ryan could argue that Mendel, like Newton, was led by empirical observation to a generalisation which included an element of invention (dominance and recessiveness) and that it is this element which turns it from a mere *de*scription into a *pre*scription.

We shall not get much further until we consider what it is that is being 'invented' or at least added to the description so as to turn it into a prescription. What is it that the prescription is telling us to do? As soon as the question is put in this way the answer begins to become clearer. We are being told to look at the empirical observations in a certain way. 'Look at the shapes of shadows or the refraction of light by prisms *on the*

[4] Although he did have to do some 'rounding off' to arrive at a ratio of 3:1 from observed ratios of 2.96:1 and 2.82:1. Indeed it has been pointed out by Sir Ronald Fisher that given the nature of the samples Mendel described it is highly unlikely that he observed even these rough approximations. There is something very odd about the whole story: see Bennett (1965).

assumption that light travels in straight lines. Look at planet-
ary motions on the assumption that bodies move at a uniform
speed in a straight line unless deflected by some force. Look
at the transmission characteristics from one generation of living
things to another on the assumption that some take precedence
over others (i.e., are dominant). Then you can apply the
theorems of geometry or probability as the case may be.'

But what is the nature of these assumptions? Can they not be
called true, or probable, or at least approximations of the truth?
At this point it is necessary to deal with the terms 'paradigm'
and 'model'. The former has been popularised by T. S. Kuhn.
Originally, it meant a pattern which is meant to be copied: then
grammarians adopted it to refer to the regular inflexions of
verbs and nouns. Kuhn, however, used it to mean the way in
which scientists 'see' the phenomena which they study. Thus
the astronomers who saw the earth as the centre of the universe
were employing a different paradigm from their successors who
saw the sun as its centre. Kuhn has, however, been justly
accused of using 'paradigm' in about six different senses, and
certainly his examples range from the geocentric assumption
of Ptolemaic astronomy to what some philosophers of science
would call 'models'.

Mathematicians and logicians use the term 'model' fairly
precisely to mean 'a set of sentences which can be matched
with the sentences in which (a) theory can be expressed, according to some matching rule' (Harré, pp. 173-4). Economists
use algebraic models to express their hypotheses concisely and
make testable predictions. In this usage a model is sometimes
no more than an algebraically expressed 'formula'. In the
philosophy of science a model is a way of visualising or otherwise thinking about what are believed to be causal sequences
of events which makes it easier for us to predict, prevent or
produce such events, or makes the sequences less surprising. An
example is the wave-model of light. But this use of the term
conceals an important ambiguity, as we shall see in a moment.

Thirdly, the term has recently become fashionable amongst social scientists and is used wholesale as the equivalent of 'exemplar', 'ideal type' or even 'approach':[5] another example of borrowing terms from the more respected sciences in order to give weight to what one is saying.

MECHANISMS

Even in the philosophy of science it is necessary to distinguish at least two kinds[6] of 'model'. It is therefore better to avoid the term so far as possible and substitute two or more terms which express more clearly what is meant. I have chosen 'mechanisms and analogies'.

Since I am using 'mechanism' in a rather special sense, let me first give an example in which it is used in approximately its ordinary sense. If an intelligent child asks 'Why did that clock-hand begin to turn after you have twisted that key a few times in that hole?' he will not be content with the merely enumerative generalisation 'Well, it always does.' To satisfy his legitimate curiosity you will have to show him, or tell him about, the working of the mechanism inside the clock: then you will have justified the statement, and given it the status of law.[7] Similarly, if asked to justify the generalisation 'I never drink Strega, and never will', I will explain that this is because I once suffered very unpleasant ill-effects after drinking the stuff, and am very afraid of repeating the experience. Since this is what

[5] As in Herbert Packer's distinction between the 'due process model' and the 'crime control model' of criminal justice.

[6] When I first made the distinction (1957) I used the term 'corresponding and non-corresponding models'.

[7] Most scientific laws apply of course to *classes* of things, and rather more general classes than clocks at that. But there is nothing wrong with applying the term 'law' to properly justified general statements about quite small classes (e.g. the known planets) or even the behaviour of presumably unique individuals: see what is said in Chapter 12 about idiosyncratic explanations.

E

passes through my mind whenever Strega is offered to me or even mentioned, it can be called in my terminology the mechanism behind the generalisation. In short, I use the term 'mechanism' to refer to any process which is believed to account for the persistent truth of a general statement, whether that process is literally mechanical, or psychological or of some other sort.

Similarly, if asked to justify the general statement that people never develop the symptoms of malaria unless they have been bitten by the anopheles mosquito a doctor will tell you that malaria results from the presence in the blood-stream of a parasite which is injected into it by the bite of the mosquito; and he will be able to show you the parasite at different stages of its life-cycle in the blood of malaria sufferers and the salivary glands of the anopheles.

ANALOGIES

On the other hand, generalisations are sometimes promoted to the status of laws not by demonstrable mechanisms but by *analogies*,[8] whether or not they are recognised as such. In effect the phenomena which are the subject of the generalisation are said to behave *as if* the underlying process were of this or that sort. Darwin's explanation of the evolution of species by 'natural selection' is based on an analogy with the way in which men produce domestic strains of animals and plants by intentional selection for breeding purposes. Darwin's inspiration was the idea that the differences between *non*-domestic species were due to a process *analogous* to selective breeding for the characteristics which differentiate species. He did not of course imagine that there had been *literal* selection, for example by God. 'Natural selection' was therefore an analogy.

Sometimes the hard sciences have to be content with an

[8] For a thorough analysis of the logical properties of analogies see Mary Hesse's *Models and Analogies in Science*.

analogy. An example cited by Harré (p. 178) is Drude's explanation of electrical conduction, which supposed that the structure of metals includes free electrons behaving *like* the swarm of molecules in a gas. Social scientists are often content with analogies, although they seldom admit that this is what they are.

A good example is the notion of 'cultural prescription' which is used by sociologists such as Robert Merton. He was concerned to explain why affluent societies have more acquisitive crimes than poor ones. His explanation was that in affluent societies the acquisition of material wealth is a goal which the culture 'enjoins', but that inequalities of education and opportunity oblige some members of such societies to adopt illegitimate means to achieve this goal.[9] But what is a culturally enjoined goal? What Merton was really saying was that members[10] of an affluent society behave *as if* they had been instructed that their main objective must be material wealth. They are not literally given this instruction; and while, as Merton pointed out, it is implied in the literature and folk-lore of the United States that material success is a worthy aim, that it is attainable by everyone,[10] and that anyone who does not seek it is in some way abnormal, this does not amount to a literal injunction.

Other notions which sociologists or psychologists have persistently employed in analogical ways include learning, labelling, marketing and drama (the last of these being involved whenever the terms 'role', 'performance', or 'scripts' are used). Most of the employers of these notions, however, have not thought about the precise status of their 'models', and have simply treated them as mechanisms. A good example is the notion of a rule, already mentioned in Chapter 3.

[9] There are of course many other ideas in Merton's justly famous essay 'Social Structure and Anomie'; to which I return in Chapter 12, but I am concerned only with this one.

[10] Or at least *males*: Merton does not discuss the interesting differences between the culturally prescribed goals of American men and women.

A rule is some sort of 'guide to action' (Harré and Secord, p. 12). It can be expressed either as an imperative or as an indicative statement. 'Look before you leap' and 'it is prudent to look before you leap' carry much the same message, although the latter has a built-in appeal to a justification while the imperative relies simply on authority. Prudence is not of course the only possible kind of justification: one may say 'It's the done thing . . .' or 'It's the Christian thing . . .' or 'If that's what you want, you'd better . . . ' or 'In this (college, regiment, union, club) we do it *this* way.'

We are concerned however not with the various possible justifications for rules, but with what is involved in following a rule. The old-fashioned view—expressed by Michael Oakeshott (1951)—is that rule-following is the conscious application of a rule. Anything else is something else: habit, imitation, automatism, or a response which is none of these but is worked out in the light of the situation as seen by the actor. As I have pointed out on p. 21 behaviour which was originally rule-following can become habitual, so that it makes historical sense to call it rule-following; but this sense must still be distinguished from the literal sense.

This commonsense point of view has been undermined partly by philosophers—especially Wittgenstein and Winch—partly by sociologists such as Goffman and Garfinkel. The philosophers argued that words (and by the same token other symbols) had meaning only by virtue of rules. To use Winch's example, it is correct to say 'Everest' when pointing to Mt. Everest but not when pointing to Mont Blanc; but correct to say 'a mountain' when pointing to either. It is incorrect in the first case because the two are not the *same* thing; but in the second case because they are. According to Winch it is the context—and therefore a rule—which determines what is to be regarded as the same thing. So using words—and presumably other symbols—meaningfully is rule-following. Anyone who has seen an infant learning to use words properly will see the force of what he is saying. We may object that once a language has been learned its use has ceased to be rule-following and become a habit: and one might point out that one teaches a baby to make the right distinctions with words not by expounding rules but by example and correction. Winch's distinction between habit and rule-following, however, is not Oakeshott's commonsense one: according to Winch behaviour which is adapted to the context is rule-following, behaviour which is repeated without adaption is habitual. Thus, I suppose, I am rule-following if I say 'Everest' on seeing a mere triangle on the map.

The contribution of Goffman and Garfinkel was to point out that although one's conduct and deportment in many every-day situations is not conscious following of any formulated rule, a departure from what is regarded as usual will elicit the sort of reactions from other people which are elicited by breaches of formulated rules.

The result of all this has been the extension of the notion of rule-following to cover an enormous variety of human behaviour which is certainly neither conscious compliance with a rule nor even the subject of rules which anyone had ever formulated expressly before Goffman, Garfinkel and their followers made their observations.[11] As MacIntyre pointed out in his review of Winch, the only example of non-rule-governed behaviour which the latter gives in his whole book is 'the pointless behaviour of a berserk lunatic.' And Harré and Secord have systematically developed the notion into a 'model' which provides an alternative to the determinism of what they call the 'mechanistic' model for the explanation of social behaviour.

This approach has attractions: chiefly that if one sees as deterministic the 'mechanistic model' offered by positivist psychologists and sociologists, then the rule model takes far better account of the many instances in which social behaviour is contrary to expectations. If someone seems to act contrary to a 'law

---

[11] This is in no sense a detraction from the value of these observations, which are often illuminating.

of nature' we feel obliged to revise the law; but if he merely
breaches a rule we are more likely to regard this as no more than
an exception, due either to the intervention of physical laws (as
when a man stumbles in the middle of a dance) or to his mis-
perception of the situation (for instance as an occasion for trying
to be funny). Occasionally we conclude that we must revise the
rule so as to take account of his behaviour (sometimes dancers
set out to make fun of the dance); but the very alternatives open
to us underlines the difference between the mechanistic and the
rule-following model.

Moreover, one can substitute the notion of a rule for that of a
natural law without necessarily ceasing to believe in the scientific explanation of human actions, as Winch argues that we
must. Harré and Secord see their 'ethogenic' models as the
basis for a non-mechanistic science of actions. This point of
view, by the way, makes it impossible to accept Hempel's
definition of scientific explanations in terms of covering *laws*,
but is quite consistent with a definition in terms of likelihood.

On the other hand, it seems important—for philosophers as
well as sociologists and social psychologists—to preserve the
distinction between literal rule-following and metaphorical
rule-following. Literal rule-following can be defined as behaviour which results from the actor's recognition of a rule.
This would include patterns of behaviour which were originally adopted as a result of rule-recognition, but are no longer
accompanied by thinking about the rule (for example, military
drill). It would also include *some* linguistic behaviour: the kind
which is learned from teachers but not at one's mother's
knee.

Other kinds of behaviour may be *described* in terms of rules
but is explicable in terms of rule-following only if it is recognised that the actor is merely acting *as if* he were rule-following.
People can be conditioned into certain linguistic patterns without realising what is being done to them.[12] The interest of such

[12] See the review of such experiments by Michael Argyle (p. 177ff).

experiments lies in the very fact that similar effects can be achieved either by expounding such rules explicitly to them or by training them as one trains animals. It is true that in some experiments some subjects become aware of the rule which is being inculcated; but that is probably because the process is more intensive than such processes are in real life: in some disciplines people acquire a preference for polysyllables from their colleagues without being aware of it. In short, a rule may be either a mechanism (when it has been recognised by the actor) or an analogy (when it has not). If so, Harré and Secord are being somewhat misleading in offering rules *as an alternative to laws*. It would be more precise to suggest that most generalisations about social behaviour have the status of laws because they are based on rules, but that the rules are sometimes mechanisms and sometimes analogies.

It certainly seems that the social sciences have difficulty in dispensing completely with analogies. There are exceptions: for example in some economic explanations which do not assume a high degree of rationality in human beings, or in psychological explanations which rely wholly on neurological mechanisms. But if introspectible events are rejected as constituents of mechanisms—as they so often are by laboratory psychologists— psychology which cannot resort to neurology must be content with analogy.[13] The methodological individualist (see Chapter 12) might well argue that sociological explainers who reject his mechanisms must similarly be content with analogies.

It is noticeable, too, in even the natural sciences that when a new sort of explanation is offered it is usually founded on an analogy. Often the new explanation consists of the application of a familiar notion taken from some other area of experience. The notion of selective breeding with a view to producing a strain with certain characteristics was a familiar one in Darwin's day; what was new was the application of it to natural species. An explanation based on a completely new sort of mechanism

[13] I return to this subject in the next chapter.

is not only harder to conceive but also harder to put into words. Either new words have to be invented or old ones used in new senses. It is much easier to begin by saying 'Well, it is as if . . .', and refine the analogy later.

For if he is fortunate the scientist's analogy is eventually found to be a mechanism. More precisely, observations suggest that the analogy is a fairly close approximation to what is actually taking place. Darwin quickly saw that his analogy of selection was a reasonably accurate picture of what happened in evolution. For he realised that if Malthus was right the reproductive rate of plants and animals must make such demands on available food that there would be a 'struggle for survival',[14] so that only those best adapted for food-getting, or defence against food-seekers, would survive.

As in Darwin's case, it is often doubtful whether the analogical element in the explanation has completely disappeared; and the most one can say is that the phenomena behave to so great an extent as if such-and-such were the case that the analogy can safely be treated as a mechanism. Thus natural selection is not literally *selection*, for it is not intentional; and one result is that different species evolve much more slowly as a result of natural selection than they do as a result of genuine selection. Again, in mechanics or geometrical optics forces or light-rays, as the case may be, are pictured as lines obeying the rules of geometry: but at a certain point the analogy breaks down, and 'rays' of light have to be thought of as 'waves' or 'quanta' instead. Indeed, a problem which has to be discussed in the next chapter is how to decide whether to regard the assumptions on which a scientific law is based as an analogy or as a mechanism. The decision is not unimportant, because unlike a mechanism an analogy may at some point mislead, and it is important to decide whether precautions against being misled are necessary.

[14] He admits that this term cannot be interpreted literally; but he could (if he had tried) have given a non-metaphorical translation.

For example, analogies can be used to rescue generalisations which are clearly contradicted by actual observation. Thus Dollard and Miller rescued the generalisation 'aggression is an invariable consequence of frustration' in the face of obvious exceptions by saying that in the case of these exceptions it was as if the aggression were there after all, but hidden and ready to burst out in an unexpected direction (i.e. 'displaced') or at an unexpected time (i.e. 'delayed').

On the other hand, an analogy can suggest directions in which we should look for further points of resemblance. The notion of selective breeding led Darwin to ask how selection could take place without being intended by anyone—that is, how there could such a thing as 'natural selection'—and thus to hit on the idea of a competitive 'struggle for survival'.

This raises the question whether an analogy which does not do this, or at least suggest some fruitful line of further investigation, is really serving any purpose. Does it, or if it does should it, persuade us to promote a generalisation to the status of a law, when all it does is to point out that the phenomena occur *as if* this or that process were taking place? Should we refuse that promotion unless the analogy suggests further possibilities which are then found to be the truth or at least tolerable approximations to it? On the whole, this seems to be asking too much. Suppose that we have observed event A to be followed by B a sufficient number of times to lead us to suspect that the generalisation 'A is (or tends to be) followed by B' should be treated as more than merely enumerative. Suppose next that it is suggested that the concatenation of A and B occurs *as if* they were linked by some process. Then so long as it is possible to make plausible suggestions as to why the process might not have taken place in those cases which A is *not* followed by B, the analogy is not a completely unsound basis on which to promote the generalisation to the status of a law, although it is not as firm a basis as a mechanism would be.

7 Confirmation

More needs to be said, however, about scientific laws, and in particular about the procedures by which our confidence in them is increased or decreased. To begin with, we must be careful to distinguish general empirical statements from statements about the mechanisms or analogies which—as argued in Chapter Six—give them the status of laws. Secondly, we must distinguish information which confirms from information which disconfirms and information which is merely consistent with a general statement. An example will make the point. Suppose that the general statement is 'Assassins—i.e. murderers of politicians—are (always/never/usually/sometimes/in x per cent of cases) female'. What sort of information about the sex of assassins would affect our confidence in such statements, and in what way?

1. Obviously the discovery of a male assassin, such as Brutus or Oswald, would completely destroy our confidence if the frequency-word was 'always', just as the recollection of Clytaemnestra or Charlotte Corday would destroy it if the frequency-word were 'never'. In short, statements of universal applicability can be disconfirmed by single instances. They need not prevent us from trying to salvage the statement by reconstructing it in a qualified form (e.g., 'modern assassinations are never the work of women' (or 'of sane women')): but we must either do so or abandon it.

2. Is the converse ever possible? Can any empirical observation ever give us complete confidence in a statement

of the 'always' or 'never' kind? Only if the class which is the subject of the statement is such that the necessary information about all its members is obtainable. If in the example given the statement were restricted to assassins *identified before 1976* it would be possible by reviewing all such assassins to be certain whether all or none were women. Such certainty might be achieved in the case of historical and other enumerative generalisations, but could not be in the case of scientific explanations, which require that their statements be of the kind that apply to both identified and unidentified members of the class for example, to future as well as past assassins. Such statements can be completely *disconfirmed* by negative instances, but never completely *confirmed* by positive instances. Even if all so-far-identified assassins turn out to be men, this does not rule out the possibility that the next one will be a woman. The most one could say on the basis of such information is that it increases our confidence in the statement. We have explored every case open to exploration which might falsify the statement, and it has not so far been falsified. Our confidence is therefore justifiably greater than it was before we had explored these cases. But it should not, in logic, be complete.

3. If, on the other hand, the frequency word is 'sometimes', how much confidence should we have in it as a result of, say, a single instance? At first we might well say that the recollection of Charlotte Corday is enough to give us complete confidence in the assertions that assassins are sometimes female. But a lot depends on what is meant by 'sometimes'. If it merely means 'not never', then certainly Charlotte Corday is sufficient confirmation. But if it means 'have been in the past and will be on future occasions (or at least one future occasion)' then she is not sufficient confirmation. The most one can say is that if it was possible

for a woman to be an assassin in the past we can think of
no reason why one should not be in the future. One could
add, too, that 'sometimes' in either sense is not disconfirmed by quite long unbroken series of contrary instances
—in this case male assassins.

4. If instead of 'sometimes', however, we want to say
something more precise, such as 'in 25 per cent of cases',
as a geneticist might, statisticians are brought in to tell us
what sort of observed frequencies should or should not
lower our confidence in such statements. Again, as was
pointed out in Chapter 5, the sort of generalisation which
is frequent in the social sciences is of the form 'X happens
more often when Y has happened than when Y has not
happened' (e.g. boys more often become delinquent if
parental discipline has been lax or inconsistent than if it has
been of other kinds[1]). This cannot even be disconfirmed
by a single negative instance: our confidence in it will be
shaken only by a long series of instances in which delinquency is not more frequently observed in boys whose upbringing has been lax or inconsistent than in the others.
Moreover, we should want to be sure that the series was
chosen in such a way as to exclude any known or probable
association between delinquency and some other variable.
Hence the enormous corpus of methodological literature
devoted to the choice of samples and controls.

It would be a mistake, of course, to imagine that our confidence in such statements depends wholly on observations
which are consistent or inconsistent with them. An inconsistent
observation usually leads not to abandonment of the statement
but to a search for some special explanation of the inconsistent
observation or, failing that, a revision of the statement so as to
take account of the circumstances in which it has been found not

[1] As observed for example by W. and J. McCord and Zola.

to hold good. This is especially so when confidence in the statement rests not only on observations but also on a mechanism which to some extent guarantees it (see the preceding chapter).

CONFIDENCE IN MECHANISMS

This brings us to the question 'What gives us (or should give us) confidence in a mechanism?' Obviously our confidence is greatest if we can actually observe the mechanism at work: if we can for example see bacteria attacking cells.

What constitutes observation is of course debatable. Is looking through a microscope 'observing'? Commonsense people, and especially those who wear glasses, would say 'Yes'. But what about an electron microscope, or a cloud chamber? Is it logical to be more convinced by seeing something than by feeling, hearing or smelling it? Suppose that we merely measure accurately the operation of some supposed mechanism, such as a magnetic 'field'?

It is possible to resolve these awkward problems by first making the distinction between mechanisms and analogies (see Chapter 6) and then recognising that in practice if not in theory it must be a distinction of degree rather than kind. In practice at least some mechanisms are simply analogies which stand up to every kind of test we can think of. Thus Darwin's 'natural selection' remains an analogy—though a very good one—because it does not work as fast as genuine selective breeding. A malaria plasmodium, however, is a mechanism because the analogy between the way in which it behaves and the way in which certain other living things behave is very close. The notion of a virus was more analogical, at least when we were unable to do more than posit the existence of a bacterium-like agent which could not be directly observed. Now that it can be observed we know that in some ways it does not behave like an independent living organism, and we are to that extent closer to a notion which could be called a mechanism. Such mechanisms might be called 'repaired analogies': that is, analogies which have been broken down at some point and been corrected.

Are there any examples of observable mechanisms in the science of human behaviour? Different sorts of people give different answers to this question. Neurologists tend to say 'Yes: we have had a certain amount of success in observing the central and peripheral nervous system at work, and also the effects on it of hormones such as adrenalin'. Most psychologists and some philosophers would concede this, but point out that it is only a fairly limited and not very interesting range of behaviour that is explicable with the help of such mechanisms: examples are epileptic fits and other 'automatisms', senile aberrations and left-handedness. Some of them would argue that so far as concerns generalisations about more complex human behaviour there are no directly observable mechanisms, only ones which can be inferred on grounds which will be discussed in a moment.

Commonsense, on the otherhand, and some psychologists and philosophers too, suggest that it is reasonable to regard directly experienced emotions, desires, calculations, impulses, reasoning as being observable mechanisms: observable, that is, by introspection. A convenient term for these is Broad's word 'introspectibilia', or its Anglicised equivalent 'introspectibles', although I do not mean to imply that all introspectibles can be regarded as mechanisms. As Harré and Secord point out.

> 'The things that people say about themselves and other people should be taken seriously as reports of data relevant to phenomena that *really exist* and which are *relevant* to the explanation of behaviour' (p. 7).

The main objection to this view seems to be that, unlike the mechanisms of a clock, introspectibles do not always operate to produce the same effects. One may feel a desire to be rude to someone and yet not do so. But a better comparison would be with the operation of a chess-playing computer which has been programmed so as to learn from its games. Its moves in identical positions will then be liable to differ, according to its intervening experiences. It would be more reasonable to argue that when we experience the desire to be rude we are observing only part of the mechanism: what restrains us may be introspectible (e.g. the reflection that rudeness would defeat some end) or it may not (e.g. it may be a lifelong training in politeness, or an unacknowledged respect for the age or status of the other person).

What is interesting is that quite a small number of observations of a mechanism at work are sufficient to give us a degree of confidence in a general statement which, if based only on instances that are consistent with it, would require a very large number of them. If we are asked to believe that pulmonary tuberculosis is contracted only as a result of close association with persons who have the disease we shall be fairly quickly convinced if shown the tubercle bacillus in sputum and lung tissues, but without this demonstration we would require a large number of instances to give us this degree of conviction.

Is it logical to be more quickly convinced by seeing the bacillus? All that this allows us to say is, in effect, 'If that is what goes on in cases of pulmonary tuberculosis, no wonder it is contracted only by close association'. Note that we must say 'if', not 'since': for we have no real guarantee that the bacillus is at work in all cases of the disease.

It may well be argued, of course, that no case of pulmonary tuberculosis has ever been microscopically investigated without discovering the presence of the bacillus. But should that give use any more confidence in the statement that the disease occurs *only* by transmission between close associates than the fact that no exception to this statement has ever been observed?

The situation is even more awkward when we are explaining voluntary behaviour. Take as an example the association between aggression and frustration which was discussed in Chapter 5. If in fact Dollard and Miller overstated the applicability of their generalisation, and frustration sometimes occurs without being followed by aggression, any mechanism which is devised to account for the connection must be one which renders it *not* inevitable but merely probable.

Again, if aggression is sometimes seen to be connected with fear instead of frustration, we must imagine at least one other sort of mechanism to account for this. If two mechanisms have to be imagined in order to account for aggression, why should there not be more than two? And if so, why should we suppose that even when aggression does follow frustration the same mechanism must always be at work? Indeed the commonsense use of introspection suggests that it is not always the same mechanism. If someone is being obstructive in negotiations I may simply lose my temper, heedless of the consequences, or I may reckon—perhaps from knowledge of his character—that a show of aggression will make him abandon his objections.

ANALOGIES

With analogies the problem is not quite the same. One does not confirm or refute them by observation: instead one seeks to discover their limitations. To what extent do organisms evolve *as if* they were being selectively bred? To the extent that certain of their characteristics—for example, length of neck or speed of movement—become accentuated over the generations. But the analogy becomes suspect when we note the slowness with which this accentuation takes place, and breaks down completely when we ask to be shown the person who is doing the selecting. Merton's analogy of culturally enjoined goals breaks down when we ask to be allowed to hear or read the injunctions. The rule-following or game analogy breaks down when people are unable to define the rule that has been broken.

To say 'breaks down' is not to imply that the analogy fails. All analogies, however illuminating from an explanatory point of view, must have their points of break-down, or they would not be analogies but mechanisms.

SIMULATION

A special kind of analogy is involved when behaviour is simulated by computers, by other machines or in non-mechanical ways. A non-mechanical example is the simulation of human decision-making by the application of rules to the information on which the decisions are based. In the English borstal system trainees are allocated to open or closed borstals by boards: a decision which is—or was—regarded as the boards' most important function. But the prison psychologists found that by using the information which the boards had about trainees' previous convictions, previous sentences, any medical or mental condition and previous treatment and any suicide attempts, they could correctly predict 85 per cent of the boards' decisions, and even predict with similar success to which of three open borstals the boards would send trainees who were considered fit for them. They could do this without being present at the boards' interviews with trainees or at the subsequent discussions. In other words, the decision-making could be simulated with a high degree of accuracy by a fairly simple set of rules (Younger, p. 246).

An example of computer simulation is Kenneth Colby's programme called PARRY, which produces a 'paranoid' style of response when the computer is subjected to questions of the kind usually put in psychiatric interviews. It was tested by arranging for eight psychiatrists to interview by teletype not only the computer but also three genuine patients diagnosed as

F

paranoid from the acute ward of a mental hospital. These psychiatrists were not told until afterwards that one of the interviewees was a computer, although they knew beforehand that a computer was in some way involved. When samples of psychiatrists were asked to distinguish the interview with PARRY from the interview with real patients they did hardly better than they would have by guesswork.[2]

Now the prison psychologists made no claim to have *explained* the decisions of the allocation boards, who would themselves have honestly denied that they were simply operating a crude system of rules.[3] And computer-using simulators of behaviour make no such claim either. Colby, however, asserts that his 'model . . . embodies an explanatory account of the complex phenomena of paranoid communication.'

Claims of this kind have been attacked by Anderson and Moore. They were chiefly concerned with the simulation of human intelligence in problem-solving; and they say for example that it is logically impossible to build a machine that will tell us which classes of problem are soluble by machines and which not, whereas human beings 'have been able to show that at least some sets of problems are unsolvable (in the required sense) by machines'. If so, machine intelligence seems to be subject to at least one theoretical limitation to which human

[2] The interviews also passed other tests of indistinguishability with some success. It is arguable, however, that PARRY was helped in passing these tests by the very fact that it was being compared with people whose responses were eccentric. Thus on one occasion the interviewer asked HOW DO YOU MEAN? and PARRY replied SHOULDN'T I BE?— a response which is so inconsequential it could pass muster only in a sample of responses for mentally disordered persons.

[3] In fact, even if they had confessed to doing so, they could have pointed to the 15 per cent of cases in which their decisions were not predictable by the rules, and could have argued that in order to identify cases which were unsuitable for the application of the rules they had to scrutinise and discuss all their cases. If so, their behaviour would not have been in the strictest sense governed by the rules. But that is by the way.

intelligence is not. They make some more general observations, however. One is that 'theories, or explanations, make *assertions*; mechanical models do not'. This is rather pedantic: the point is that successful mechanical simulation *encourages* assertions of the kind which Colby makes. Another of their observations is that from similarity of performance we cannot infer similarity of structure: mechanical diggers are not built like men, nor aeroplanes like birds. Again they seem to miss the point: mechanical diggers and aeroplanes are not designed to *simulate* navvies or birds, but to dig better than men or carry loads which birds could not. Colby's programme, in contrast, is designed not to improve on human conversation but to imitate the strangely imperfect responses of a paranoid person.

More relevantly, all that Anderson and Moore are prepared to concede is that 'the virtue of attempts at mechanical simulation is that they *may*, with luck, suggest the kind of theoretical problem which, if solved, would explain both the original behaviour and that of the mechanical analogue'. Thus attempts to build flying machines led to an understanding of the laws of aerodynamics which explained both the successful flight of birds and the eventually successful performance of aeroplanes. This is a substantial concession; but it probably would not satisfy Colby, who claims that his programme 'embodies an explanatory account' and justifies this by *equating* some of the rules in his programme with the 'lawlike generalisations' which are essential to an explanatory account.

Unfortunately, although he gives plenty of examples of the rules in his programme he does not indicate which of them are the equivalent of laws. Some of them are mere 'housekeeping' rules or technical instructions to make sure that an interview can proceed. Thus if the interviewer is silent the computer is told to select a prefabricated response from its 'exhaust' list, and if the silence continues to go on doing so until each response has been tried once, after which it is to end the interview. Colby is presumably not implying that such rules are the equivalent

of any laws. He probably had in mind the rules which make
the computer select responses according to the level of its
'anger', 'fear' and 'mistrust', variables which can be increased
or decreased by the nature of the interviewer's remarks. 'Anger'
decreases more rapidly than 'fear', which in turn decreases
more rapidly than 'mistrust'; but all are decreased by such remarks as 'You are right' or 'I understand you', and increased
by such remarks as 'You don't seem very alert'. When they
reach a certain level the computer refuses to discuss its central
delusion (which is that it is being persecuted by the Mafia for
non-payment of horse-racing debts).

In fact it is misleading to think of the rules of the programme
as the equivalent of whatever laws govern the responses of
paranoid patients. What Colby ought to have said is that he
could formulate laws about their responses which should inspire
some degree of confidence not merely because they describe the
pattern of these responses fairly well but also because the pattern
is *as if* the patients were following the rules of his programme:
in other words that he can support his law-like statements not
by a mechanism but by an analogy. The greater the success of
PARRY in passing indistinguishability-tests the more we feel
that the processes which paranoid patients respond as they do
must be something like the prescriptions of the programme.

On the other hand, suppose that we were offered another
programme which also mimicked the responses of patients
with persecutory delusions (let us call it PERCY) but which
was based on a set of rules of which some differed markedly
from PARRY's. Suppose further that its responses to certain
kinds of questions or statements were better than PARRY's, and
that there was no respect in which its performance was inferior.
Obviously we should prefer it to PARRY, and say that its rules
were more likely to resemble the mental processes of paranoia.
Suppose, however, that in some respects PERCY was superior,
but in others inferior. Suppose, too, that there seemed to be no
way of combining the differing rules of the two programmes.

This should worry only those who had been misguided enough to regard PARRY and PERCY as rival *mechanisms*. If we recognise that they are only analogies we can say without any unease that in some ways paranoid patients behave in some ways as if they were PARRY and in some ways as if they were PERCY.

8 The inadequacy of scientific explanations

In Chapters 3 and 4 I mentioned several kinds of explanation of human behaviour which can be regarded as non-causal, and therefore by ordinary standards non-scientific. What has now to be faced is the extreme point of view which holds that we should not be seeking explanations of any kind, but something called 'understanding'.

This point of view is summed up by Michael Phillipson:

'One distinction between the two approaches which is very relevant to the analysis of crime concerns their goals: one goal of natural scientific investigation is to locate *the* cause or the *causes* of phenomena, while the goal of the other perspective is not 'the causes' but rather certain kinds of 'understanding' or interpretation of social phenomena. This understanding is qualitatively rather different from causal explanation; essentially it seeks to understand the processes by which actors arrive at their particular pattern of choices and describe the actors' perceptions of the limits of these choices . . .' (pp. 28–9).

Although Phillipson is here distinguishing his approach from 'causal' explanation, and especially causal explanations of the naive kind which assume that the explanation of theft is the same the world over, he does at times seem to be saying that we should not be attempting any sort of explanation, but instead should be trying to 'understand' or 'interpret' deviance.

The distinction between explanation of a scientific, causal sort and 'understanding' is not of course new, but goes back to the nineteenth-century German philosopher-historian, Droysen, and is the subject of a huge corpus of literature. It is usually treated, however, as a distinction between two kinds of explanation: for example, Georg von Wright more or less equates it with the distinction between causal and teleological explanation. The assumption, however, that 'understanding' is not a kind of explanation at all is a rather newer notion.

Phillipson's notion of 'understanding' seems to include the usual element of 'empathy'. To understand one must to a certain extent try to create in oneself the thoughts and feelings of those in whose behaviour one is interested, although Phillipson would no doubt admit very readily that one cannot know to what extent one is succeeding, and whether the imputed thoughts and feelings are anything like the subject's own. The notion also includes the concept of 'typical' responses to 'typical' situations: that is, responses which are shared with others. Thus, says Phillipson:

'... the sociologist accepts that every individual has his own unique perspective, experiences and interpretations, but he is concerned with the essence of what is common to the members of any group in their interpretations.

For example, do the boys who occasionally go on shoplifting expeditions together, in spite of the differences in their individual emotional responses of fear, detachment or excitement, share common interpretations of these events? Do they typically give the same kind of explanation for their activities? Do their explanations vary according to whom they are explaining the events, so that their typical explanations to their mates differ from their typical explanations[1] to their parents, which in turn differ from their typical explanations[1] to juvenile court magistrates or inquisitive sociologists? Posing this kind of question

[1] The reader must not be confused by these references to 'explanations'. Phillipson means that one must listen to these explanations even if what one is aiming at is not, on his view, explanation.

suggests that any event can have several typical meanings and that such typical meanings will depend very much on the context and relationship in which they are given. A comprehensive understanding of the meaning of any kind of event depends on the sociologist's ability to describe these different meanings and show how they are congruent or in conflict with each other . . .' (pp. 39–40).

This is the only concrete example which Phillipson gives of the 'understanding' which he wants to substitute for explanations. It is clear, however, from the first quotation that what he is doing is equating 'explanation' with 'scientific explanation', so that in his terminology any other kind of statement which ends our surprise cannot be an explanation.[2] The second quotation makes it plain that in place of scientific explanation he is offering us a 'what' explanation. We are being instructed to identify 'the essence of what is common to the members of any group in their interpretations': that is, to classify what they are doing according to their interpretations. But, as was argued in Chapter 4, a classificatory explanation is really no more than a hint at one or other of the genuine kinds of explanation, which the giver hopes the questioner will not to have spelt out in full.

A more precise and less monopolistic exposition of the nature and function of understanding is offered by Rickman who defines it formally as

'. . . the grasping of some mental content to which an expression points; it is, therefore the primary cognitive pro-

---

[2] There is also a hint in the first quotation that a dash of *narrative* explanation may be required: we are told that we must sometimes understand 'the *processes* by which actors arrive at their particular pattern of choices' (my italics). There is nothing wrong with explanations which are a mixture of different kinds, so long as one does not fight shy of recognising the ingredients of their explanatory nature.

cess through which the subject matter of the human sciences is given to us; it pervades these disciplines and is indispensable to them; its successful conclusion on the highest possible level is the goal of the human studies. The orientation towards understanding thus characterises the disciplines concerned with man and distinguishes them from the physical sciences'.

In Rickman's language one merely 'comprehends' the working of machines, however man-like:[3] understanding is reserved for mental content and is achieved only through the interpretation of 'expressions', a term that 'covers anything which expresses something, or refers to something. It includes words and signs of any kind, as well as what may be called expressive behaviour (such as weeping)'. Despite his claim, however, that it is 'the goal of the human studies' he is quick to emphasise that it is not the only 'process' used in the human studies, nor is it 'self-sufficient' or 'comprehensive'; and he blames positivists for foisting this claim on the 'understanding' school (although anti-positivists such as Phillipson must surely take the main share of the blame).

What is interesting is that even Rickman does not go on to discuss what the other 'processes' are which complement understanding. I suspect that if 'explanation' had not been a dirty word in the vocabulary of his school he would have used it. For it is possible to grant, quite ungrudgingly, that a student of human behaviour must understand the states of mind which accompany different sorts of behaviour, and yet go on to ask that he should explain them, whether in a narrative or a scientific sense. If I, walking out of my common-room, take an umbrella from the stand and someone asks why I did so, the first thing to be clear about is whether I thought is was mine or not. If the questioner is told that I regarded it as my own property, he may not continue to want to know why I took it.

[3] He does not discuss whether one can 'understand' animals.

But then again he may: for example if I am merely leaving the room for a short time (the answer may be that too many umbrellas have been stolen from the common-room recently, and that I am being careful with mine). If, on the other hand, the questioner is told that I did not regard it as my property, he is even more likely to want an explanation.

In other words, if what the understanding school are maintaining is that when the explanandum is human behaviour it has not been completely defined until the mental states of the actors have been included in the definition, they are in the right. But those who go on to argue that to describe the behaviour with understanding makes explanation in some way beside the point have so far failed to show why. The most that they can argue is that an understanding description[4] of a transaction often of itself removes curiosity: but not always. What they have not seen is that it is up to them to show why, when someone is puzzled by some human action, and has been given a description of it which makes him 'understand' it, it is illogical for him to say 'But why did he do what he did in that state of mind?' For example, 'Why, if he knew that the umbrella was not his, and was in no immediate need of an umbrella, did he take it?' In short, the valuable point which the understanding school are making is that when the explanandum is human behaviour every effort should be made to describe it in such a way that the states of mind of the actors are precisely defined. But to describe an explanandum properly is not to make an explanation illogical, or *inevitably* superfluous.

---

[4] Even so, Braithwaite's definition, cited on p. 1, would make such a description an explanation: but I am not relying on this definitional argument.

9 The inappropriateness of scientific explanations

There is, however, a group of philosophers who argue that *scientific* explanation is inappropriate to human actions.[1] One of the curiosities of Rickman's and Phillipson's books is that they ignore this very group which one would expect them to cite in their support. The reason may be that the understanders draw their ideas chiefly from a nineteenth-century German tradition, in which it was merely argued or assumed that scientific explanation was *inadequate* in the human studies, whereas the argument that it is *inappropriate* is the more recent product of an English group.

The leading exposition of this point of view is Peter Winch's *The Idea of a Social Science*. In the same year, however, R. S. Peters published an equally important book, *The Concept of Motivation*, which, in common with Winch's book, maintained that 'if we are in fact confronted with a case of a genuine action (i.e. an act of doing something as opposed to suffering something) then causal explanations are *ipso facto* inappropriate' (p. 12).

Neither Peters nor Winch question the propriety of explaining in causal terms the sort of behaviour which we usually regard as purposeless or unintentional, although as Peters himself points out, one of Freud's achievements was to make us see as purposeful some kinds of behaviour which we had hitherto regarded as merely 'caused'. They are quite content to leave

[1] They distinguish 'actions' from 'acts' (or 'behaviour'), by using 'actions' to refer to purposeful behaviour, 'acts' or 'behaviour' to refer to movements which seem automatic (e.g. an eye-blink) or purposeless (such as doodling), or externally caused (as when one is knocked over).

breathing, sleeping, bowel movements, eye-blinks and knee-jerks to physiologists, and conditioned reflexes and habits to psychologists (Winch p. 62). Even where *actions* are concerned, Peters concedes that causal explanations are relevant. They can state some of the necessary conditions for the occurrence of an action: for instance if a certain part of the brain is damaged one cannot speak. By the same token, they can account for some, but not all, individual differences in performance: for instance, as one's brain ages the speed and precision of one's speech may decline. And they may explain a breakdown in performance, as when brain damage causes a person to use inappropriate words. But, say Peters and Winch, the complete explanation of the performance of an *action* cannot be wholly *causal*.

At this point it seems necessary to distinguish Winch's central argument from one which he interweaves with it. The central one is concerned with the prediction of human action. It goes like this. What social scientists are mainly concerned with, it says, is social behaviour, which is behaviour that *means* something to other people. Meaningful behaviour[2] is *ipso facto* rule-governed (p. 52), in the sense in which the term can be applied to a language or a 'way of life'—even that of an anarchist, though not that of a 'berserk lunatic'. The test of whether a man's utterances or acts are rule-following is not whether *he* can formulate the rule but whether it makes sense to distinguish between a correct and incorrect way of doing what he is trying to do. Rule-following is more than mere habit, since it involves modifying one's behaviour to suit the circumstances (e.g. if the transaction is with a foreigner one may use simpler language, or flourish money in a way which would be insulting to a compatriot). A man's knowledge of how to use a language (or be-

---

[2] and 'therefore all specifically human behaviour' adds Winch. His sweeping statements about rule-governed behaviour have been ably criticised by Alasdair MacIntyre in an essay also called 'The Idea of a social science' (1971), which is the broadest and best attack on Winch known to me.

have on a committee) differs not merely in complexity but also in kind from a dog's ability to perform a trick for the man *understands* the rules he follows.

What social scientists are trying to do is to predict how people will act in accordance with *reasons*, which implies acting *intelligibly* in terms of the modes of behaviour familiar in the society to which they belong. But, asks Winch, is prediction of this kind exactly like prediction in the physical sciences? Prediction involves—*inter alia*—recognition of regularities in the occurrence of events, and consequently the catagorising of separate events as similar.

In the physical sciences such similarities are simply a matter of agreement between the *investigators* who study the phenomena; but the social scientist, says Winch, must know what his *subjects* regard as similar before he can talk about regularities. Following a rule involves recognising similarities in situations, and what counts as similar under one rule might not count as similar under another. Thus an Oxford don who is invited by another don to dine at his college may regard this either as a friendly piece of hospitality or as an attempt to secure his support for some scheme; and he will adjust his behaviour accordingly. As Winch puts it, it is the *subjects'* rules, rather than the *scientists'*, which 'specify what is to count as "doing the same kind of thing".'

Thus an observer, O, of N's behaviour who wants to predict what N is going to do in a certain situation must familiarise himself with the concepts in terms of which N views the situation (for example, whether he sees the dinner as hospitality which ought some day to be returned or as a bribe for his vote). Even if O does use the same concepts as N, however, the latter may still do something different from O's prediction. If this happened in the natural sciences it would imply some sort of mistake on O's part: 'false or inadequate data, faulty calculation, or defective theory'. According to Winch this would not follow in the prediction of *meaningful* human behaviour.

'Sometimes' says Winch 'even if O knows with certainty the rule which N is following, he cannot predict with any certainty what N will do: where, namely, the question arises of *what is involved* in following that rule, e.g. in circumstances markedly different from any in which it has previously been applied. The rule here does not specify any determinate outcome . . . though it does limit the range of possible alternatives; it is made determinate for the future by the choice of one of these alternatives and the rejection of the others—until such time as it again becomes necessary to interpret the rule in the light of new conditions' (p. 92).

At this crucial point Winch fails to give an illustration of the sort of situation which he has in mind.[3] Just before the quoted passage, however, he gives an example of predictable rule-following, in which N is known to be following instructions to start with zero and add 2 until reaching 1,000. If O knows that N has just written down 104 he will be able to predict that he will next write 106. If we adapt this sort of example we might suppose that N was following an instruction to write down the square roots of all integers below a certain number, and we might imagine O's difficulty if asked to predict what he would do about the square root of 2. Yet even in such a case O would probably act like a natural scientist and ask for more data. Does N know enough arithmetic to be aware of the peculiarity of $\sqrt{2}$? Does he have the help of a computer? What square roots has he worked out so far? If the answers are, respectively, no, yes, and 'no square root that ran to more than four places of decimals', O might predict that N would write 1·4142. If on the other hand N knows quite a lot of mathematics and O is aware of this, O will probably predict that N will ask what he is supposed to do about $\sqrt{2}$. The more he knows about N and the ways in which he has hitherto followed

---

[3] It is not clear why he specifies a situation in which the choice of an alternative limits future choices. It is only in legalistic situations that this holds good; and legal decisions *are* rather predictable.

the rule the better he will be at predicting what he will do in a difficult situation.

A more favourable example for Winch, however, might be the moral rule that requires promises to be kept. Let us suppose that N, with O's knowledge, promises Q never to reveal some fact which Q wishes to remain secret. Q dies, and it becomes clear to N that keeping his secret is harming people whom Q would not have wished to harm. How can O predict whether N will keep it or not? Again surely he would reason like a natural scientist, and reflect on what he knows or can find about N. Is N an obsessional promise-keeper? Has he a tendency to gossip? How serious in N's eyes would be the harm in keeping the secret? Does N realise that the secret is in fact known to quite a number of Q's friends who are bound by no such promise? If the answers are no, yes, not very and yes, O will predict, sensibly, that N's lips will become unsealed. If the answers are yes, no, very and no, he will predict the opposite. Admittedly other combinations of answers would make prediction more chancy, and O might be tempted to say 'He will give it away only if he gets very drunk when in the company of the people affected'.

Perhaps, however, Winch is thinking of a situation in which N is faced with an almost arbitrary choice, with no obvious guiding principle of a rational kind. He may, for example, have been taken to some horce-races and feel compelled to place bets like the rest of his party although unlike them he knows nothing about the sport. How will he place his bets? Again from knowledge of N it might be predictable that he will simply ask his friends for advice or that he will more cautiously pick favourites or boldly go for outsiders, or alternate between these policies according to his wins or losses. In this situation O is quite likely to make mistakes; but the difference between it and situations in which his predictions are likely to be correct is one of degree, not one of kind. Information about N's state of mind and previous behaviour will be relevant—that is, will somewhat reduce the likelihood of mistakes.

In short, it is very difficult to imagine a rule-governed situation in which 'data', to use Winch's term, are completely irrelevant, although this is what his argument seems to require. The central fallacy, however, seems to be Winch's apparent assumption that if O cannot predict with certainty he is not fulfilling the criteria of a natural science. Yet we saw in Chapter 1 that the explanations of the natural science do not always yield such predictions, for the reasons given by Scriven. So that successful prediction, while it increases our confidence in an explanation, is not a *sine qua non*.

Suppose that O were to say 'God knows what N will do in this situation: it's a bit of a toss-up. But if you tell me what he does decide to do, I'll tell you why he made that choice'; and suppose that on being faced with O's explanation N agreed that it was correct. Is this not a close analogy to Scriven's engineer, who can explain why a bridge has collapsed, but could not have predicted the collapse? Like so many philosophers, Winch has an idealised image of the natural scientist's abilities and a narrow view of his aims.

What we must now consider, however, is a more widely held view, which does not assume that causal explanation must make accurate prediction possible. This can be summed up in the statement that 'Motives and reasons for actions are not causes of actions.' Since this appears clean contrary to commonsense, the arguments for it must be fairly set out and discussed. There are four of them:

1   *because causes and effects are different events, whereas the description of many (if not most) motivated actions is not complete without the specification of the motive.*[4]

---

[4] Although the discussion is usually about *motives*, what is said seems to apply to *reasons*, although the reverse is not always true.

An example is a signal made by a motorist who sticks his arm straight out of the car's window. To describe it as 'a signal' is to specify his motive, which is to signify to other motorists that he is about to turn. But two situations have to be distinguished here. In one, he realises that his turn may take other motorists by surprise, and consciously decides to signal his intention. In this case there are undoubtedly two events, for between the decision and the action something may intervene to prevent the action: his arm may be seized affectionately by his child in the back seat. The fact that a full description of the action of signalling involves a reference to his motive does not necessarily mean that two separate events which were causally related did not occur.

The situation, however, which bothers the philosophers is the one in which the motorist simply sticks his hand out of the window, intentionally but without previously thinking to himself 'I must signal', yet if asked by his child in the back seat 'Why did you stick your hand out of the window?' could truthfully say 'I was signalling that I was going to turn'. It is in this situation that it is plausible to deny that there were two distinct events: signalling and wanting to signal. In some cases, of couse, it would be plausible to say that the motorist was so well trained or conscientious that signalling had become a *habit*. The fact that he told his child that he did it because he wanted to signal would not necessarily exclude this possibility, for his explanation might be a loose way of saying 'I learned long ago to do that when I am about to turn in order to tell other drivers what I am going to do'. (The fact that *some* habits—such as scratching one's head when puzzled—cannot be rationally justified does not of course mean that *no* habits can be). The possibility that it was an habitual act is relevant, because philosophers do not deny that such acts are caused, and there is something habit-like about any act which, though accountable in terms of a motive or reason, is not preceded by a decision to perform the act. Yet some philosophers seem to distinguish an

G

intermediate type of act, which is not preceded by a decision, yet is not quite a habit. It is this type which makes it most plausible to argue that the action and the motive (or reason) are not distinct events. On this view, actions are not *explained* by describing causal processes, but *expounded* by having their meaning clarified. Ayer's answer to this is that 'causal relations should be regarded as holding between facts rather than events, where 'fact' is understood in the wide sense in which true propositions of any form can be taken as expressing facts.' This is not a merely opportunistic debating point, for it has other consequences to recommend it. For example, it makes it easier to understand why we are willing to apply the term 'cause' to something which immediately precedes the explanandum in time, or to something which is contemporary with it, or to something which did *not* occur.

2   *because a motivated action is (usually or always?) a rule-following act, so that it can be said to be more less correct in terms of the rule.*

The implication of this argument seems to be that if we admit its truth it excludes the possibility that actions have causes. Like Ayer and MacIntyre I cannot see this implication. Why should an action not both be a correct way of doing something and have a cause? After all, a computer can be said to perform correctly or incorrectly in exactly the same sense. Ayer goes on to suggest that perhaps all that is intended by the arguments is that, in our present state of knowledge, relating an action to a rule is a better way of 'accounting for it' than 'trying to subsume it under dubious causal laws'. But, says Ayer, the actor's recognition of the rule he is following is as much a causal explanation as any other sort. It is true that Winch and Garfinkel could point to situations in which the actor followed a rule without previously saying to himself 'I am following this rule', and without being able even to formulate the rule, yet may feel that he did the proper thing. Such behaviour, however, is plausibly regarded as habitual, imitative or in some other way conditioned; that is, as caused.

3   *because it does not seem to be possible to point to causal laws connecting motives with actions.*

For, so the argument goes, an action A may be performed from a motive M on a given occasion without its being true that whenever A is performed the actor was motivated by M, or conversely that whenever the actor is motivated by M he does A. The most that can be said is that there is a tendency for M to be associated with A. The same could be said, however, of many a cause-and-effect relationship in the natural sciences. As has been pointed out in Chapter 5 it is only in laboratory conditions that X is invariably associated with Y. If one is to use this argument one must be specific about the conditions under which the event or action might happen, and the possible alternatives. Thus it would be naive to state as a causal law that a man who is insulted by another will retaliate by another insult. He may be a man of strong Christian principles combined with self-control. He may be afraid of being physically attacked. He may enjoy planning a subtler revenge. He may not wish to be involved in a public quarrel. But the more possibilities of this sort one can exclude the more probable it becomes that he *will* make an insulting retort. Is this so different from the statement that, the humidity being what it is, there will be rain tomorrow unless for instance there is a heavy thunderstorm in the night or a warm wind from the south? As for the choice of alternatives and appropriate ways of responding there are machines which have alternatives and even preferences for one alternative. A roulette wheel can acquire a tendency to prefer certain numbers if one or two of its slots are very slightly widened. Undeniably the relationship between motive and action is more complex than this, perhaps even than causal relationships in meteorology; but nothing has been said to show that it is not a causal one.

4 *because the real cause-effect relationship holds between physiological events, such as the activation of neurons and the electrical stimulation of muscles.*

This is an argument which is not used by Winch or Peters, although it is discussed rather inconclusively by Ryan (Ch. V). The reason may well be that it appears to be destructive not only of the sort of explanation of actions which Winch and Peters want to destroy, but also of any sort explanation except a physiological one. Winch and Peters do not want us to give up the idea of *explaining* human actions in non-physiological terms: what they want us to do is to give up explaining them in cause-effect language.

One could obviously dismiss it by pointing out that it rests on unproven, perhaps unprovable, assumptions about the relationship between physiological and mental events: for example, the assumption that what we refer to as 'feeling angry' or 'understanding a sentence' do not bear some fairly close relationship to the events which, according to the physiologist, constitute the 'real' causal chain. We say 'lightning causes thunder', when most of us know that the scientist would describe the process in terms that made no reference to sights or sounds; but we assume that what we call 'lightning' is seeing one part of this process, and what we call 'thunder' is hearing the other part. Similarly, even if we believe that the 'real' causal processes are physiological, may we not justifiably say 'I got angry because I understood that he was insulting me'? The argument seems to be that we must not: and it must therefore assume that words such as 'rage' and 'understanding' cannot be treated, even roughly, as names for physiological processes in the way in which we treat 'lightning' and 'thunder' as names for meteorological events. And of course there is no evidence for this sweeping assumption.

There is, however, a less extreme interpretation of the argument. It may allow us to make general statements, such as

'People who hear certain words or phrases addressed to them become angry' or 'People do not behave in that way unless they are angry'; but may simply be pointing out that these are mere general statements, not laws, since they lack any sort of guarantee that they will continue to hold good. What the argument may be saying is that *the only mechanism which will guarantee this is a physiological one*. If that is all that is being maintained, it need not worry social scientists very much. Just as we may continue to say 'lightning is always followed by thunder' so long as we realise that only the meteorologists can give an account which will *guarantee* this, so social scientists can be allowed to generalise in mental terms so long as they realise that only the physiologist can provide a mechanism that will confer the status of *laws* on what they say.[5]

[5] There are other, more extreme, arguments which ought to be mentioned, although they are not taken as seriously as those which have just been discussed. One is the discredited teleological explanation of actions or social phenomena, mentioned in Chapter 4. Another is the view that human actions are not determined, but governed by a 'free will'. As Ayer points out, this simply assumes the truth of what it is meant to prove: that actions have no causes (so that they cannot have motives—or anything else—as causes).

10 Explaining what exactly?

So far this book has been concerned with explanations. In Chapter 8, however, it became clear that in certain situations a sufficiently precise description of what is being explained could be a substitute for an explanation: and there are other ways in which the sort of explanation demanded may be affected by the definition of the explanandum. The next three chapters are therefore concerned with the nature of the explananda of criminologists and other students of misbehaviour.

What this chapter is *not* about is the long-standing demarcation dispute between rival intellectual trade-unions about the proper subject-matter of criminology. The main point of the chapter is that to define the subject-matter of a discipline is not to define its explananda. Nevertheless, it is necessary to review briefly the series of rickety arguments by which the present muddle over explananda has been achieved.

In the nineteen-thirties it was still being argued by writers such as Michael and Adler that since empirical investigations required a precise definition of what was being investigated, and since the criminal law provided a precise definition, the only sensible boundary for the subject-matter of criminology was breaches of the criminal law and those who broke it. But the variability of what is prohibited by the criminal codes of different states, or at different times in the same state, worried social scientists such as Catlin and Sellin who felt that the subject of a science ought to be determined by some intrinsic *differentia*, and not by the vagaries of legislatures. Sellin thought that he had solved the problem by extending the criminologist's field of study to what he called 'conduct norms'; that is, 'group rules' which treat certain kinds of conduct as being contrary to the interests of a social group; and he proposed the title 'ethology' for this redefined discipline.

As Sutherland (1947) pointed out, however, conduct norms also vary according to the group which one has in mind. If the variability of the boundary set by the criminal law is a sound reason for abandoning it, conduct norms suffer from the same variability. It is true that, as Sellin had said, they are usually based on a stronger consensus than many legal prohibitions; but consensus can and does change. Indeed, had Sutherland been writing today, he might well have argued that conduct norms differ more between social groups, and alter more rapidly, than the contents of criminal codes. This has not, however, prevented Sellin's argument from being uncritically revived by latter-day sociologists such as Michael Phillipson (p. 57).

Meanwhile, however, the terms 'deviation' and 'deviance' had been introduced as generic descriptions of the subject-matter of the new discipline. Lemert, who was largely responsible for this development, was anxious to find a value-free substitute for the notion of 'pathology' which was explicit or implicit in the approach of the pre-war social scientists who concerned themselves with 'social problems', but which had been discredited by sociologists such as Wright Mills.

Lemert expressly borrowed the term 'deviation' from statistics, and used it and 'deviance' to mean 'other than normal in the statistical sense' (1951: 27 & Glossary). There are still sociologists, such as Wilkins (Ch. IV), whose reasoning assumes that relative infrequency is an important—if not a defining—characteristic of deviance. Lemert himself, however, seems at first to have taken the view that its essential characteristic was that it consisted of an infringement of some norm of behaviour which was more than merely statistical, and was consciously adhered to by most of those to whom it applied: the infrequency was merely an indication of the existence of a norm. Later in the same book—and in later publications—he became more concerned with what he called 'secondary deviance': that is, the effect upon an actor's behaviour of being detected in (primary) deviance and 'labelled' accordingly.

The effect, however, of Lemert's emphasis on the labelling of deviants was to suggest to sociologists, notably Kitsuse and Becker, that even primary deviance should cease to be regarded as a 'quality of the act'—e.g. infrequency or infringement—and instead be defined as a consequence of the application of rules and sanctions to an infringer by others. Indeed for some modern interactionists, as we shall see, it does not seem to be essential that a *rule* be in anyone's mind: merely that the behaviour should be the subject of some sort of adverse reaction by others.

What Becker and others were rightly emphasising was the well-known fact that not all behaviour which infringes rules (a) is detected or (b) is attributed to identified individuals or—even if (a) and (b) happen—(c) results in the necessary adverse reaction. The circumstances may be regarded as justifying it (so that it becomes a non-infraction) or as mitigating it (so that it becomes a pardonable infraction). Conversely, individuals may be *wrongly* identified as infringers of rules. One must therefore distinguish between an action which is, in the abstract, an infraction and an actor who in practice is treated as an infractor.

The interactionist school has posed problems for itself. Some of them are trivial, although they have been the subject of serious discussion. An example is the question whether there can be 'secret' deviance, known only to the actor (Answer; yes, if he himself labels his action as an inexcusable infraction). Of the same order of difficulty is the question 'Can the creation of a rule render actions which preceded it retrospectively deviant?' (Answer: it depends on the attitudes of those who apply the rule).[1]

There are however difficult questions. Becker (p. 8) attacks the rule-definition of deviance by pointing out that someone whose action breaks the rules of one group may be acting in

---

[1] See the case of R. v. Shaw, briefly described on p. 98.

accordance with the rules of another group. But this objection applies with equal force to the reaction-definition. One group may react adversely to the very action which is approved—indeed regarded as the only correct thing to do—by another. How does one tell which group one is to refer to (in the technical language, how does one define the reference group)? Does one ask the actor which group he thinks he 'belongs to'? What if he says 'Both', as a football fan might if asked whether he belonged to Manchester United or Manchester? And suppose he asks 'What do you mean, "belong"?' Or does one ask members of each possible group whether he belongs to it? And what if it is his very behaviour which leads a group to say 'No'? The only safe answer is a relativistic one: that a person is deviant *only in relation to groups which treat him as such*, whether he 'belongs' to those groups or not.

But what sorts of adverse reaction are to count as rendering someone deviant? Occasionally people actually refer to someone as 'a deviant' or 'deviate'; but—sociologists apart—the term is not common outside the U.S.A., and even there tends to mean a person whose sexual behaviour is abnormal. What other labels, then, confer the status of deviance? 'Sinner', no doubt. ('Saint' too, says Wilkins, for whom every extreme on a statistical distribution must have its opposite.) 'Schizophrenic', says Scheff: but what about mere depressives or neurotics? Dwarfs and giants, say Dinitz, Dynes and Clarke: but what about the skinny or obese? Vagrants, drop-outs and hippies, says almost everyone.

In short, what is the quality of a reaction which makes a person deviant? Must it be one of moral disapproval? Not if we include saints as Wilkins does, or schizophrenics as Scheff does. Must it be at least adverse? After all Wilkins *could* argue that one is made to feel uneasy by saintliness even if one respects it. However that may be, there are many kinds of adverse reaction on one person's part to the behaviour of another: censure, fear, hate, contempt, ridicule, disgust, intellectual opposition,

disappointment, irritation, embarassment, impatience. What
have they in common but adverseness?

Perhaps the reaction should be defined as one which has
detrimental effects on the relations between the labelled individual and the other members of the reference group? This
would allow us to include the situation in which the group goes
to the length of expelling a member, or denying that he belongs
to them. Goffman points out, however, that groups sometimes
react protectively to deviants, as when a person whose behaviour
or sayings makes him ridiculous is affectionately 'adopted' as
the group clown. Saints too have a privileged rather than an
ostracised existence, at least when they attain recognition as
saints. No doubt these awkward categories of 'in-group' or
'licensed' deviants, as Goffman calls them, could be excluded
by definition, so that some sort of limit could be set to the kinds
of reaction which qualify.

Yet this would not be an end of the problems. The ethnomethodologist would intervene to criticise the distinction between actions which *in the abstract* are infractions of rules and
those which are treated as such in practice. Douglas points out
that, quite apart from the problems involved in abstract rules—
such as conflict between them—there are considerable uncer-
tainties as to their meaning and their application in specific
situations. 'Even when we do know what the rules are in the
abstract, we cannot predict from this how the rules will be interpreted in any given situation. . . . The necessarily problematic nature of rules means that they must always be interpreted,
or their concrete meanings constructed, for any concrete situation' (p. 199).

It is not easy to make out exactly what this ethnomethodolo-
gical criticism amounts to. Is he arguing that the distinction
between the rule in the abstract and the interpretation of it in
a specific situation is artificial or meaningless? Yet by ethno-
methodological criteria it cannot be if we are able to argue
about rules in abstract, although it might be if we found it

impossible[2] to carry on such arguments without bringing in specific situations. Is he arguing that the general statement of a rule, such as 'the dishonest appropriation of another's property with intention to deprive him of it permanently is theft, and punishable with imprisonment etc.' is of no help whatsoever in predicting what will happen if I walk off with a stranger's brief-case in his presence and without his permission? Not even Winch, who made a similar point (as we saw in the previous chapter) some 14 years before Douglas, would have been so sweeping. Or does Douglas merely mean that there are border-line situations in which it is hard to say whether the owner will shout 'Stop thief!' or do something else to have me arrested? If so, the point is inconclusive. The argument rests on the ambiguity of the word 'problematic', so frequently used by ethnomethodologists. When they apply it to specific situations they mean that the rule does not always tell you how those involved will behave; but when they are talking about rules in the abstract they use it as if it meant 'of no predictive value at all'.

A more awkward question is 'Must a *rule* be in the minds of the reference group if the actor is to be categorised as deviant, or is it sufficient that they merely react unfavourably toward him?' When Thomas Brown wrote

I do not love you Dr. Fell,
But why I cannot tell;
But this I know full well,
I do not love you Dr. Fell.

was this the sort of reaction which, if shared by the other members of Christ Church, would have made the Dean a de-viant? Or would he have been so only if they had been able to give reasons for their dislike? Sellin's 'conduct norms' have sur-vived in the writings of most sociologists of deviance—including

[2] We certainly find it *easier* if we are allowed to talk about specific situations; but hardly *impossible* if we are not.

ethnomethodologists—as 'rules'. One of Schutz's most important contributions (see p. 19n) was the observation that far more
of our social transactions are rule-governed than had been
thought, even if we are aware of many of the rules only when
they are formulated for us.

If so, perhaps the problem of defining the sort of adverse
reaction that makes behaviour deviant can be solved by requir-
ing that the adverseness be attributable to the fact that the behaviour is regarded as infringing a rule? This would not imply
that all rule-breaking is deviant: only rule-breaking which leads
to an adverse reaction.[3]

But it is not always easy to say when an action is regarded as
an infraction of a rule. Just as there are difficulties in deciding
whether a person is obeying a rule so there are difficulties in
deciding whether reference groups are reacting because a rule
has been broken, or are expressing their unease by formulating
a rule for the first time in a way which prohibits the action.
This can happen even in the criminal law. When a Mr. Shaw
published a *Ladies Directory* in which London prostitutes
advertised their services, he was convicted of, *inter alia*, 'con-
spiracy to corrupt public morals'. Until that case most criminal
lawyers would have hesitated to say that such an offence
'existed', and the Court of Criminal Appeal did say that there
was no such offence. The House of Lords, however, decided
that there was.

The same sort of thing happens far more often outside the
courts, although it is of course less easy to point to specific
examples. Symptomatic of it are phrases such as 'One doesn't
do that sort of thing', which is plainly an inchoate *post facto*
formulation of a rule to express a condemnatory attitude to
some action. In some cases reference groups obviously find it
very difficult indeed to formulate the rule which deviants are
breaking. Vagrants and hippies are an example, yet any defini-

[3] Including an adverse reaction on the part of the actor: see what is
said about 'secret deviance' above.

tion which excluded them from the category of deviants would hardly be acceptable to sociologists.

Since virtually all sociologists of deviance now include mental illness within their subject-matter, the attempt to define it in terms of rule-breaking is especially interesting. According to Scheff, we give this label to people who infringe what he calls 'residual rules': the sort of rule-breaking which is not necessarily[4] illegality, immorality, bad manners, unprofessional conduct, cheating or a breach of any other special set of rules, but contravenes some unclassifiable rules of deportment which Scheff therefore calls 'residual'. Examples are: ignoring those present, while talking as if one were conversing with an unseen, unheard person (without using a telephone or radio) or laughing while conversing with someone about a sad or serious topic, such as genocide. These may or may not be breaches of manners (according to the circumstances); what matters is that they breach ill-defined rules that dictate how one should converse. Similar rules govern other kinds of deportment.

There is no doubt that Scheff is not merely saying that it is invariably this sort of rule-breaking which draws attention to, or leads to an eventual diagnosis of mental illness: for him it is what defines the symptoms of mental illness (p. 40). In any case, however, it is obvious that neither is true. Excessive compliance with rules, such as the rules of hygiene, can be the reason for a diagnosis of obsessional states, which can be reconciled with Scheff's view only by the sophistry of arguing that the obsessional is breaking the old Greek maxim μηδὲν ἄγαν ('don't carry things too far'). How abstract can a rule be? Again there is the question 'In what sense is the person who converses with unseen, unheard people breaking a rule?' Did anyone, before Scheff came along, really formulate a rule? If so what was it? If it was simply 'One doesn't talk to unseen, unheard people' then it was clearly an inadequately formulated rule, which failed to take into account telephones, radios and

---

[4] But of course it may *also* be illegal, immoral etc.

prayer. If it was 'One doesn't talk to non-existent people' what about actors like Joyce Grenfell, whose object is to entertain in just this way? Two points seem clear: the 'rules' which the mentally ill are said to infringe are unformulated, and secondly, if they were formulated, would have to include some very general reservations: for example, 'one doesn't do that *without good reason*'.[5]

It seems obvious that there are literal rules (of the kind which are promulgated in writing or by word of mouth) and metaphorical rules, which are formulated after the event to justify some adverse reaction. Sociologists of deviance can define some of their subject-matter in terms of adverse reactions to breaches of literal rules, but some only in terms of adverse reactions to conduct which breaches no literal rule, only a metaphorical one.[6] In which case the concept of rule-breaking does not really support an all-embracing definition.

I hope that this digression has illustrated both the value and the problems of the contributions made by sociologists of deviance. In particular, it must have convinced the reader that if the reason for abandoning law-breaking as a definition of the subject-matter of a discipline was its 'cultural and temporal relativity' (Phillipson, p. 57), sociologists of deviance have jumped out of the frying-pan into the fire.

This is not an attack on the notion of deviance, even if it lacks precision of the notion of a criminal offence.[7] In some

---

[5] To which R. D. Laing might well reply 'And the "mentally ill" have good reasons!'.

[6] This is not quite the same as the distinction in Chapter 6 between literal and metaphorical rule-following.

[7] A criminal offence is an act which infringes the criminal law of the jurisdiction within which it is committed. Thus adultery may be a criminal offence in one jurisdiction but a matrimonial one or merely a breach of a moral rule in another one. Attempts to confuse the issue by talking about 'crimes against humanity' are playing on metaphors. As for the problem raised by retrospective legislation, this is a moral one, and does not undermine the definition.

ways it is a good thing that criminologists have been induced to interest themselves in non-criminal behaviour. The social processes which decide whether various sorts of behaviour are treated as criminal or not are interesting subjects for descripttion and explanation. Again, almost every sort of criminal behaviour has non-criminal counterparts, which must be taken into account by would-be explainers.

The confusion which needs to be cleared up is between the subject-matter of a discipline and the subject-matter of explanations. It has been and still is assumed[8] that the two must be identical. But there is no logical necessity which links them: merely the assumption that explanatory theory is so important that it dictates boundaries. Even if one holds the extreme view (discussed in Chapter 13) that a single theory will explain all crime, or all deviance, it does not follow that what can be explained by this should define the subject-matter of a discipline. After all, as has just been said, social scientists ought to be, and are, interested also in the processes by which different types of behaviour become categorised as criminal or deviant, or the opposite.

Again, some social scientists, including some criminologists, are more or less pure describers. Unless their descriptions are theory-laden to a naive extent, there is no logical reason why the distinctions which they involve should claim to be distinctions between explananda. Indeed, a descriptive criminologist might well say, for example, 'I am going to carry out a descriptive study of the conduct which is comprised in the legal definition of bigamy, because I suspect that it is very heterogeneous'. This would not imply any assumption that he was proposing to study a single explanandum: if anything[9] it would imply the contrary.

[8] See for example what used to be Chapter 2 but is now Chapter 1 of Sutherland's *Principles of Criminology*, where the confusion has survived revisions for a quarter of a century.

[9] 'if anything' because it might have no implication either way. He might limit himself to distinctions based on the sex of the bigamist,

Once we have got rid of the notion that the subject-matter of criminology or the sociology and psychology of deviance can be defined as an explanandum or collection of explananda, the nature of these explananda becomes less difficult to see; and this is the subject of the next chapter.

whether the non-bigamous spouse knew the union was bigamous, and whether the bigamy had been prosecuted.

11   Surprise

We can begin by asking what it is that makes people seek an explanation of any particular occurrence or action. Almost always it is surprise: an encounter with something contrary to expectation. But what makes us expect one thing rather than another? Usually[1] some sort of regularity in our experience. We expect something similar to what we have previously encountered in similar circumstances. It does not matter whether this expectation is rational or merely the result of conditioning: it is so. We expect similarity and are surprised by dissimilarity.

But when asking for an explanation we must be prepared to make the reason for our surprise explicit, and specify or at least hint at the dissimilarity which is surprising us.[2] If we can see a man wheeling a lawn mower up and down a strip of grass and ask 'Why is he doing that?' our respondent may be puzzled, and say 'What do you mean? He's cutting the grass.' We should have been more explicit, and said 'Why is he cutting the grass when it was cut only yesterday?', the implication being that it is highly unusual for someone to cut the same strip of grass two days running.

It is of course perfectly possible to be genuinely surprised by regularities, whether in nature or in artefacts, such as roulette wheels. Tides, seasons, bowel movements and the similarity of parents and offspring are examples, although we tend to forget the stage at which we found them surprising. Intentional behaviour abounds in instances: hobbies, metaphorical addictions

---

[1] That is, unless we are in the sophisticated position of having some theory which tells us what to expect even if we have not experienced it.

[2] A point made by Hart and Honoré (p. 33), though in a different context.

H

(say to gambling), traits such as quarrelsomeness or shyness. Artefacts may behave with surprising regularity: an example is a roulette wheel which has been 'fixed'.

But what about the familiar unsurprising regularities? What makes scientists try to explain them? The answer in some cases is that they were trying to explain an irregularity, but in doing so had to explain a regularity. Mendel *began* by trying to explain differences in the characteristics of peas, and ended by outlining the model which has been developed to account for both similarities and dissimilarities between parents and offspring. Sometimes, of course, the scientists are not so much explaining as discovering and describing regularity: $G = \mathrm{Mmk}/\mathrm{D}^2$ is Newton's particularly neat way of describing the regularity in the strength of gravitation, but it is not an explanation. Sometimes the scientist wants to alter or make use of a regularity, as when agriculturists try to produce better breeds of animals or vegetables. It cannot be denied, however, that scientists are often motivated by the kind of surprise which in Chapter 1 I called artificial and chronic, and which we distinguish from natural surprise by the name of 'curiosity'.[3]

The next point to be made is that the same action can be several different *explananda*, according to the questioner's knowledge (or belief) about its context, as the following example shows:

a. I see Smith, a school-boy, entering a betting shop and putting some money on a horse, and I ask him for an explanation. But if I am to get the sort of explanation I want I must make it clear whether I am surprised by his choice of horse, or by the size of his bet, or by the sight of a bet being

---

[3] Thomas Kuhn suggests that 'normal' science, when it is not merely describing, consists of 'puzzle-solving'. It is not aiming at any revision of its fundamental paradigms (see p. 54), merely trying to work out how to apply its accepted paradigms and laws to the explanation of some hitherto unexplained regularity.

placed by someone whom I believed to be opposed to betting on moral grounds, or by a flagrant breach of the school rules.

b. let us suppose that Smith's bet was not against his moral code, was of an amount which he could afford, and was based on a choice which was by betting standards rational, so that what surprised me was his breach of the school rules. I might then be satisfied by his explanation that being a new boy he did not know the rule. But next time I catch him betting my question must be 'Why, when you know it is against the rules, do you bet?' The explanation might be that he thought the chances of detection were small, or the penalty tolerable.

c. suppose, however, that in spite of being caught twice in succession and fairly severely punished he is again found betting. The question must then be 'Why, when he knows the chances of punishment are high, does he persist?' The answer may be that he feels under some compulsion. He may feel obliged to challenge any rule which he regards as unreasonable; or he may be a compulsive gambler.

And so on: the questioner's definition of the explanandum differs according to his knowledge about the odds, the school rules, Smith's moral code and Smith's experience. Morover, each different definition of the explicandum makes certain types of explanation admissible or inadmissible. The question 'Why did you bet such a large sum?' or 'Why did you put it on an outsider?' is not answered by the reply 'I didn't know it was against the rules', just as the question 'Why did you disregard the rule against betting?' is not answered by the statement 'I had inside information about the horse'.

It is a vague appreciation of this which makes school-masters, police and other rule-enforcers approach 'Why?' questions with caution. Their first question is much more likely to be 'What

do you think you are doing?': a very sensible application of
verstehen. For it is only when they have some idea of the rule-
breaker's definition of what he thinks he is doing that they can
proceed to define the explanandum with some degree of precision.

In other words, knowledge that this or that behaviour is
illegal does not by itself guide us automatically to a sensible
definition of the explanandum. To ask 'Why did you bet when
it is against the law (or the school rules)?' is sensible only if it
can be assumed that the prohibition is known by people of the
category to which the questioner has mentally assigned the
transgressor, and that they either to some extent endorse the
rule morally or fear the consequences of detection and consider
the chances of it substantial. But it is only in law (and not in all
codes of law[4]) that every sane adult is presumed to know all
the prohibitions to which he is subject. As for endorsement, not
even the law presumes that this is universal. And where the
consequences of transgression are concerned, we know that
many people are optimistic—often realistically so—about their
chances of getting away with offences or are prepared to risk a
mild penalty such as a fine.

This is not to say that it is never sensible to ask 'Why did
Smith infringe such and such a prohibition?' It may be a prohibition which he must have known, and probably endorsed;
or it may be understood between questioner and answerer that
the circumstances were such that Smith must have realised he
was likely to incur a severe penalty or stigma. But legal definitions are not designed as definitions of explananda, and it is
only by good luck that they can sometimes serve us as such.

By the same token, however, it is equally unsound to ask
'Why did Smith do that if it is deviant?' In the first place, the
man in the street does not treat deviance as a property of actions
in the way in which he accepts 'illegality' or 'criminality' as a

---

[4] In the Norwegian criminal code, for example, this presumption is
subject to sensible limitations.

property. It is only sociologists—and as we have seen not all sociologists—who assume that people think in this way. Who would dream of saying to someone 'Why were you deviant last night?' or even 'Why did you do that when you knew it was deviant?' What one might well ask is 'Why did you make a fool of yourself last night?' or 'Why were you so bad-mannered (or inhospitable)?' or more specifically 'Why did you tell your guest it was time he went home?'

Secondly, as with law-breaking, one may be surprised by one form of it but not by another. Just as we are surprised when a middle-class housewife is caught shop-lifting, but not when she is caught breaking the speed-limit, so we are surprised when a politician makes himself ridiculous but not when he breaks promises.

Thirdly, it is often necessary to be even more specific about the context of the action in order to define what is surprising than it is in the case of law-breaking. Theft is the dishonest appropriation of property belonging to another with the intention of permanently depriving the other of it. But what is rudeness? Definitions in dictionaries do not tell us how to recognise it: they merely give us verbal equivalents. If, at a party, I say 'You'd better go home' to a woman who is a little drunk, whether I am being rude or not depends on our relationship, our respective roles (for example, whether I am her host or her husband) and even the tone of my voice and my facial expression. Again, whether she was 'drunk' depends on the situation and the standards of the people at the party. A slight slurring of the speech may raise eyebrows at a diplomatic reception. At the other extreme, Herbert Wechsler tells a story of a witness in a trial who was asked whether a man lying on the floor had been drunk, and replied 'No, I saw him move his hand'.

Fourthly, we may be just as surprised by an action which is not deviant in any sense in which the word is used by sociologists, but is simply 'out of character' so far as the particular actor is concerned, or—to be more precise—inconsistent with what we suppose his character to be. It is surprising when a man whom we regard as financially careful speculates heavily on the stock exchange, or makes a very generous donation to charity; or when a bibulous man refuses a glass of his favourite drink.

On the other hand, suppose that an action is not only out of character, but also known to the actor to be deviant and illegal, as when a teetotaller becomes drunk and disorderly in a public street. An explanation which simply said that he thought there were no police around, or that people would be tolerant because it was Christmas Eve, would not satisfy us, because we should want to know why he had drunk any alcohol at all.

In short, there is no principle which allows us to say that a definition of an action as contrary to some convention, conduct-norm or standard of rationality is more satisfactory for explanatory purposes than a definition of it as illegal or out of character. What defines it satisfactorily as an explicandum is a statement of what it is that surprises us, whether it is the infringement or observance of a law, a convention, a moral obligation, a dictate of prudence. 'Law-breaking' and 'deviance' are no more than generic names for some but by no means all of the actions which may (or may not) call for explanation according to the observer's perception of the action and its context. The same would be true of any generic name for actions which are out of character, or surprising in their context, though not necessarily illegal or deviant: perhaps the nearest thing to such a term is 'aberration'.

Moreover, if we think about aberrations of behaviour as explananda we realise that they cannot be just descriptions of the behaviour, but most include—either expressly or by implication—*the assumptions which make the behaviour unexpected.* We ask Smith 'Why are you placing bets when you know it is against the school rules?', thus making more less explicit the assumption that he like other boys knows and obeys the rules. Or we may ask 'Why are you driving on the left-hand side of the road?', and leave unstated, because taken for granted, the clause '. . . when you know that we have reached a country in which they drive on the right?' If the explanandum is the *observance* of a law, convention, moral obligation, dictate of prudence or such-like, we shall probably feel obliged to make an assumption more or less explicit, and ask 'Why are you being more law-abiding (or whatever) than usual today?'

This is not merely a point about usage: what is being emphasised is that if the definition of any given explanandum is to be complete and not elliptical it must include the assumptions which led the questioner to demand an explanation. Secondly, where law-breaking or deviance is concerned, those assumptions will usually include a clause of the form 'when the actor knows that his action is illegal (or unconventional, imprudent, ridiculous or whatever)'.

12 Kinds of explananda

The second point to be made is that until one has some idea of the form which an explanation is going to take the definition of what one is trying to explain must be treated as *provisional*. For the explanation will probably turn out to explain both a little less and a little more than the original envisaged explanandum. In order to illustrate the point without too much complexity it is necessary to take as an example some sort of conduct which is fairly specific, and in the case of which it is not too naive to imagine that a single explanation might be sufficient. (Consequently it would, for instance, be ridiculous to take 'homicide' or 'personal violence' or 'shop-lifting' or 'dishonest acquisition' as illustrations). Perhaps the best choice is what is usually called 'indecent exposure', although it is sometimes known as 'exhibitionism'. This is an offence committed by men who expose their penis to a non-consenting woman, usually a stranger, but without assaulting her.

Let us suppose that a psychologist or psychiatrist, after studying a sample of indecent exposers,[1] and perhaps comparing them with properly selected controls, is able to put forward a single explanation in terms of upbringing, feelings of sexual inadequacy and so forth. He is then likely to come up against at least two observations. One is that there will be at least a few of his exhibitionists to whom his explanation cannot plausibly

[1] Let us suppose that he has been able to collect a sample which is not confined to detected cases: my point has nothing to do with possible bias of this kind.

be applied.[2] If he is a thorough investigator he will look for some other explanation for these cases, and perhaps find one. It is said, for example, that indecent exposure is sometimes committed by subnormal males not for deep psychological reasons but because it is their notion of an overture to normal sexual intercouse. If so, the investigator will recognise two explananda instead of one, and will redefine them as 'exhibitionism by subnormal males' and 'exhibitionism by males within the normal range of intelligence'. These too may may prove to need further refining, for he may find that some adolescent males of average intelligence and without psychological abnormality act in this way as a joke.

More interesting still is the possibility that the explanation which seemed plausible for the majority of cases might also turn out to account plausibly for conduct other than the offence of indecent exposure. It might be found for example that some of the controls, although selected because they had never exposed themselves to a strange woman, seemed to have had the same sort of upbringing and feelings of sexual inadequacy as the indecent exposers. On investigation of this group it might be found either that they *did* expose themselves, but to consenting women such as wives or girl-friends, or else that they admitted to having impulses to expose themselves to strange women. If so, the explanandum would need to be redefined so as to include *more* than the original definition of it.

I am not suggesting that whenever a social scientist finds that his explanatory hypothesis seems to apply to some situations in which the explanandum has not occurred he must invariably redefine his explanandum. This sort of finding is very common[3]

[2] Donald Cressey is the only criminologist known to me who was fortunate enough to find that his explanation applied to 100 per cent of his sample (in his case embezzlers: see his book *Other People's Money* (1953).

[3] Cressey (see p. 100) might well have encountered it if he had tried to collect a control sample of people in positions of trust who had *not* embezzled the money entrusted to them.

in studies of human behaviour, and is often used as a refutation
of explanatory hypotheses by people who have not thought
about the logic of field-work outside the laboratory. The fact
that some sons of criminal fathers do not become criminals[4]
does not refute the hypothesis that a father's willingness to
break the law is likely to predispose his son to do so; for all
sorts of other factors—such as a strict mother—may interfere.
But if the investigator has done his best to exclude factors likely
to affect his findings in this way—as some scientists are able to
do in laboratory experiments—and still encounters such findings, he is bound to wonder whether he is dealing with more
than one explanandum.

Sociologists have of course long been aware of the need to
sub-divide popular classifications of their explananda, whether
in legal, ecclesiastical or other codes of conduct. Durkheim may
well have been the first, and is certainly one of the few, to say
explicitly why this seems necessary:

'à un même effet correspond toujours une même cause'

Thus, he says, if suicide appears to have more than one cause
it is because there are really several kinds of suicide.

What Durkheim states as a fact of nature is of course better
regarded as a methodological principle: that the explanandum
should be so defined that all instances of it are susceptible of
the same explanation. For sometimes commonsense seems to
contradict Durkheim. Take the example used on pp. 37–8, in
which a motor-car overturns on a bend in the road. As we saw,
it may overturn at exactly the same point on the bend, and come
to rest in exactly the same position, but in one case the explanation may lie in its speed, in another it may be the force of the
wind, in another a sudden swerve to avoid an oncoming vehicle
or pedestrian. Commonsense says that the same thing can have

---

[4] The language is loose; but there is no need to be more precise when
dealing with this crude sort of reasoning.

different explanations. The logician, however, replies that this is all very well as an everyday way of talking about what happens, but it will not do if explanations are to be tested. How could one attempt to confirm (or more precisely disconfirm) an explanatory generalization about the maximum speed at which a vehicle of a certain weight could round a bend of a certain radius if one did not define the situation so as to exclude high winds, unexpected pedestrians and so on? If Durkheim meant that this is one of the 'Rules of Sociological Method', and indeed of scientific method in general, he was right. More precisely, there is no harm, and some benefit, in the methodological principle that the definition of an explanandum should be such that explanations of all instances of it are in terms of the same concepts and laws. The fact that this will sometimes involve distinguishing explananda solely by reference to types of explanation, as Durkheim sub-divided suicides, admittedly introduces an element of circularity into the definition; but since it is merely a rule for constructing definitions this does not matter.

That Durkheim's statement of the principle, however, can—and did—inspire nonsensical approaches to the explanation of misbehaviour will be demonstrated in the next chapter. Meanwhile, a possibility which he did not discuss was that an explanation might explain more than the explanandum which the explainer had in mind, although this sort of serendipity must be the pipe-dream of almost every kind of scientist—or at least every scientist who is motivated by intellectual curiosity rather than a mere desire to predict, prevent or produce (p. 2). To take Durkheim's own example, some suicides, we are told nowadays are best explained as desperate attempts to communicate some very strong feeling to one's nearest and dearest. But so are some attempts and some pseudo-attempts at suicide; and indeed some completed suicides are best explained as suicidal demonstrations—that is, communications—which have more or less accidentally become actual suicides.

In short, the definition of the explanandum must always be

treated as provisional until the explanation or explanations have been formulated.[5] It follows from this, however, that explainers of misbehaviour—or of any behaviour for that matter—must take an interest in behaviour which falls outside the definition of their explanandum but is similar to it, in case their explanations should turn out to be plausible explanations of more than their explanandums. Thus, to return to the example of the exhibitionist, the would-be explainer of this should interest himself in legitimate as well illegitimate exhibitionism. Explainers of criminal violence should study legal violence or more precisely, violence which is not perceived as illegal; for example not only fighting in the streets but also fighting in the boxing-ring, the ejecting of troublesome customers from bars and dance-halls, forcible law-enforcement and so on. This is one more reason why the definitions of the criminal law cannot be adequate definitions of the field of interest of would-be explainers.

The next point concerns explananda which consist of regularities in behaviour. Before going on to it, it is worth reminding ourselves of the distinction drawn in Chapter 2 between probability- and possibility-explanations. The explanations which we often accept—either quite happily or *faute de mieux* —for particular actions are of a kind which merely tell us how it was psychologically possible for the actor to act as he did, and not why his action was very likely, let alone inevitable. Sometimes, it is true, we receive a probability-explanation when we would have been satisfied with a possibility- one. We may ask how so-and-so could have brought himself to resign the

---

[5] This is probably the point which Albert Cohen (1959) was making when he said that ' . . . any definition of a theoretical field is necessarily tentative, because homogeneity for theoretical purposes is a hypothesis that is verified only when a unified theory has actually been evolved to account for the variation in question. . .' But if so he failed to see (i) that it is a methodological principle, not an hypothesis; and (ii) that it applies whether a single 'theory' or more than one 'theory' is being offered.

Ministerial post for which he had longed, and be told that he had been offered the choice between resignation and dismissal. We should probably accept without discussion the general proposition that politicians regard resignation as less damaging to their reputations than dismissal, which makes it extremely probable[6] that if offered a choice a politician would choose the former.

Note that this sort of explanation makes use of a generalisation, in this case about politicians. It tells us that this is the way in which politicians regularly behave, and suggests the reasoning which is the underlying mechanism. It is thus a crude example of a scientific explanation. Sometimes, of course, all we are given by way of explanation is a generalisation: a statement about a regularity. 'He (the Minister) is like that: works for something but throws it away when he's got it'. Or 'He's easily discouraged, and gets out of situations in which he doesn't achieve immediate success'. The regularity may be familiar or it may be surprising, according to our experience and knowledge. We may have come across plenty of such people, or none. If it is surprising, we shall want an explanation of it, thus in effect saying that we are not satisfied with it as an explanation.

The regularity is often stated in a way which is explicitly or implicitly comparative. 'He is more likely than most politicians to resign out of discouragement' is explicitly comparative. 'He resigns about once a year' is implicitly comparative, implying as it does that this frequency is above average. It is this sort of regularity which is most likely to call for further explanation.[7]

Such comparative generalisations are by no means always about individuals. They may be about groups of individuals. 'Conservatives resign from office more frequently than Socialists'.

[6] But not of course inevitable: he might feel that his reputation was high enough to cast discredit on the Prime Minister who asked him to resign.

[7] The same is true where inanimate objects are involved.

'Non-motoring homicides are more frequent, in proportion
to population, in the U.S.A. than in Britain'. 'Adultery is
commoner in the thirties and forties than in younger or older
age-groups'. 'Public drunkenness is more often seen in Camber-
well than in Belgravia'. The distinction between comparisons of
individual frequencies and of group frequencies seems an obvious one, but is hardly even mentioned, let alone discussed, in
the literature of criminological explanation. The only such discussion I have noticed is a short passage in the 1947 edition of
Edwin Sutherland's *Principles of Criminology* (pp. 8–9), where
his exposition of his theory of differential association led him to
write:

'. . . The preceding explanation of criminal behaviour
was stated from the point of view of the person who en-
gages in criminal behaviour. It is possible, also, to state
theories of criminal behaviour from the point of view of
the community, nation or other group. The problem, when
thus stated, is generally concerned with crime rates and
involves a comparison of the *crime rates* of *various groups
or the crime rates of a particular group at different times*.
One of the best explanations of crime rates from this point
of view is that a high crime rate is due to social disorganisation. The term 'social disorganisation' is not entirely satisfactory and it seems preferable to substitute for it the term
'differential social disorganisation'. The postulate on which
this theory is based, regardless of the name, is that
crime is rooted in the social organisation and is an expression of that social organisation. A group may be
organised for criminal behaviour or organised against
criminal behaviour. Most communities are organised both
for criminal and anti-criminal behaviour in that sense the
crime rate is an expression of the differential group organisation. Differential group organisation as *an explanation
of a crime rate must be consistent with the explanation of*

the criminal behaviour of the person, since the crime rate
is a summary statement of the number of persons in the
group who commit crimes and the frequency with which
they commit crimes.

The point might have been taken up by criminologists and
sociologists of deviance if Sutherland had developed it more
fully and been clearer in his own mind. By simply saying that
the explanation of a crime rate must be 'consistent' with the
explanation of an individual's criminal behaviour he gave the
impression that it does not matter much which the explainer
has in mind. But it does. First, there is the elementary point
that it is quite possible for some type of behaviour to be commoner in one group than another although no single member
of either group could be said to be prone to it. Even if no Conservative minister had ever resigned more than once it might
still be true that resignations were commoner amongst them
than amongst Labour ministers. It is true that, even so, there
might be a 'Conservative personality', which was likely to lead
to resignation in situations in which the 'Socialist personality'
would not; but there could be explanations which did not imply
any greater tolerance of resignation amongst individual Conservative. Conservative policies might create more situations
in which ministers' principles were at stake, or, in other words,
might yield more 'narratives' each different but each explaining why an individual resignation was psychologically possible,
without implying any relevant psychological differences between members of the two parties.

Secondly, the phrase 'consistent with' was used ambiguously
by Sutherland. If all he meant was that explanations of differences in the group frequencies of, say, theft must not *contradict*
explanations of the existence of theft-prone individuals, this
seems unexceptionable. But we know, of course, that he had
unquestioningly accepted a narrow version of methodological
individualism, and believed that the explanation of group rates

must not merely contradict but also be reducible to explanations of individual propensities (that is, be expressible in terms of such explanations) just as the phenomena studied by chemists are explainable in terms of atomic physics. There is nothing illogical about this viewpoint: it simply begs one of the controversial questions about sociological explanations.[8]

Although I am not at the moment discussing the tenability of the view that explanations of all social phenomena are reducible in this way, it is worth pointing out that some forms of explanation begin as explanations of individuals who misbehave more often than others, while others begin as explanations of group rates of misbehaviour. Sutherland's own theory of differential association began by asserting that individuals become delinquents because their associations with other individuals have been such that in their experience 'definitions favourable to violation of law', have been 'in excess of definitions unfavourable to violation of law. Such an hypothesis (for Sutherland never put it to the test, and attempts to do so have been inconclusive) does not lead inevitably to the proposition that there are no forms of 'delinquency' (to use Sutherland's term) which can be explained in other ways, still less to methodological individualism: but since Sutherland regarded an explanatory theory as acceptable only if it explained *all* forms of 'delinquency', he was psychologically bound to arrive at this position.

An example of explanations which begin with group rates is Merton's version of 'anomie', to which I have referred briefly in Chapter 6. His original explicandum was the high and increasing level of acquisitive crimes in affluent societies, a phenomenon certainly contrary to expectation. He argued that members of such societies feel that they are expected to be successful in terms of material possessions, but that the inferior education and environment of lower class males makes legiti-

---

[8] See Steven Lukes' brilliantly concise review of the literature on methodological individualism.

mate means of achieving this goal more difficult for them than for members of higher social classes. They may solve this problem in different ways. Some make the *means* their *end*, and get satisfaction out of correct performance of a task, however unremunerative or pointless it is (this is called 'ritualism'). Some choose *illegitimate means* to the prescribed goal (this he called 'innovation', but it is more often known as 'dishonesty'). Some adopt more easily attainable goals, such as the pleasure obtainable from music, sex, drugs: this is 'retreatism'. Finally, some try to change the whole system, and are called 'rebels'.

As can be seen from this very bald summary, his explanation branched out so as to cover more than acquisitive crimes, although he was too sensible to regard it as a criminologist's stone (see p. 127). But was it reducible to explanations of individuals' innovative, ritualistic, retreatist or rebellious behaviour? Merton did not address himself to this question, but others offered answers to it. Some posited a psychological state in the individual, called 'anomy' (by MacIver) 'anomia' (by Srole) or, more loosely, 'maladjustment' (by Riesman et al.) or 'alienation' (by Nettler). Others, notably Cloward and Ohlin did not find it necessary to posit a psychological state which reflected a society's degree of anomie, but instead suggested that differences in the social organisation of under-privileged areas resulted in the 'recruitment' of individuals to different types of delinquent organisations, although they finally had to bring in psychological differences (in intropunitiveness and moral inhibitions) in order to account for retreatism and ritualism. On the whole, the history of 'anomie' demonstrates that while an explanation of differences in societies' crime-rates (or 'deviance-rates' for that matter) *may* be such as to call for an explanation of differences in the behaviour of individual members of societies, it does not necessarily dictate the form of such an explanation, and indeed may leave a good deal of latitude in this respect.

There may well be types of behaviour, of course, which are

I

such that an explanation of high group rates *must* make use of the assumption that the group contains individuals who behave in this way with unusual frequency. The more abnormal the behaviour the more plausible this is. If children are sexually molested with unusual frequency in a particular locality we expect to find a relatively small number of individuals who are responsible, and whose tendency to behave in this way is what really demands explanation.

At the other extreme, however, are types of behaviour which may be unusually frequent in certain areas or social groups not because some members of these groups are especially prone to it, but because it is the sort of thing which most people are liable to do under circumstances to which these areas or groups are particularly subject. Some areas of cities are plagued by illegal parking not because they harbour people with a particular disregard for the law but because they have stations, supermarkets, and other places to which normal people want to drive, but do not provide enough facilities for legal parking. Robbery, looting and some other forms of acquisitive crime increase in frequency when law enforcement agencies are weakened—for example by a policeman's strike, or a race-riot.

Such explanations still adopt the approach of methodological individualism. There can be situations, however, in which methodological individualism can be sustained only in a very diluted form, as Steven Lukes has pointed out. Some kinds of misbehaviour are manifested by people who would not normally indulge in it themselves, but do so in certain group situations. Personal violence and damage to property by football crowds, demonstrators or people celebrating some success are examples. Competitive situations seem to produce dishonesty (such as fouls in ice-hockey, cheating in bridge tournaments) violence (for instance amongst spectators at football games) or risky driving (as in motor rallies).

The point is that while all the forms of behaviour which have just been instanced can be described as the behaviour of individuals, in some cases the explanation must in one way or another refer to the situation of the group as a whole, and cannot confine itself to the personalities or case-histories of the individuals. To say in such cases that the explanation of group rates must be 'consistent with' the explanation of the individual's behaviour is subtly misleading: it *is* the explanation of the behaviour of the individuals, but an explanation which cannot be completed without talking about the group as a whole.

THE PARTICULAR ACT

An explanandum which is hardly ever mentioned nowadays, let alone discussed, is the single infraction, for as everyone knows a single event must be treated for the purpose of scientific explanation as merely an instance of a general statement. But this is yet another example of the way in which we ignore other kinds of explanation. As we saw in Chapter 2, a single event can be the subject of a possibility-explanation, and this is so even if it is regarded as a unique event.

Even if one wants a scientific explanation, however, particular acts raise problems which are not entirely trivial. In the first place, there is usually a choice of generalisations where human actions are concerned. When a woman is found stealing a coat from a shop, and on investigation it emerges:

i. that she has very little money and no other coat;
ii. that she is on bad terms with her husband, by whom she feels neglected; and that he is a very respectable man, who feels deeply disgraced by her theft;
iii. that her mother was a fairly well-known and successful shoplifter.

we may feel that we are presented with a choice between three fairly well-worn types of scientific explanation, each based on a different generalisation:

I*

a. she needed a coat (it was a cold winter) but hadn't the money to buy one. In such circumstances people resort to dishonest acquisition. (Let us call this, perhaps crudely, an 'economic' explanation);

b. she wanted to revenge herself on her husband, and at the same time recapture his attention. In such circumstances women will do self-damaging things if they know that it will make someone else concerned about them. (Let us call this, whether fairly or not, a 'clinical' explanation);

c. she had been fond of her mother, and been rather impressed by her resourcefulness in meeting the family's needs by shop-lifting. Children, even when adult, will often adopt patterns of behaviour which they have observed in parents, especially of the same sex. (Let us call this, again with apologies, the 'child-rearing explanation').

This illustrates the sort of uncertainty which often confronts probation officers, psychologists or psychiatrists who are expected to give causal diagnoses of individual acts of law-breaking. In such a situation it might conceivably be possible, perhaps as a result of conversation with the woman, to eliminate all but one of the possible explanations. If not, we may be offered a statement of the form 'All three factors contributed to her conduct'. But this is ambiguous, and might mean

a. that each was a *necessary* condition; that is, that but for each of them she would not have stolen the coat. It is hard to imagine what evidence would justify this assertion, although not hard to imagine evidence that would negative it;

b. that whether or not any factor was *necessary*, none by itself would have been sufficient. It is easier to imagine evidence which would justify a statement of this kind. It may be possible to establish with reasonable certainty that in spite of her upbringing she has not hitherto shoplifted or that in spite of her upbringing and a long history of marital neglect she has not done so. But as the example illustrates, when one of the conditions has existed almost as long as the individual one cannot hope to find strong evidence that without it another conditions would not have been sufficient.

c. that these three factors together make up one sufficient set of conditions, but that there are other possible sets and that none of these factors would figure in all those sets (in other words that none of the factors was a necessary condition and none by itself sufficient). This is compatible with (b) but says more.

IDIOSYNCRATIC EXPLANATIONS

By the time one arrives at (c) it seems that the diagnostician is either asserting much more about the individual than that individual's history justifies or basing his assertions on information about a class of individuals (such as British wives). The latter is not illogical, so long as he recognises two facts. One is that the generalisations about the actions of British wives or any other class of human beings are probabilistic, or more precisely of limited and imprecise applicability (see pp. 42–3). The second fact is the possibility (and legitimacy) of what I call 'idiosyncratic generalisations' where individuals[9] are concerned. Sometimes we seem justified in saying 'Oh yes, she behaves like that whenever . . .'[10]

It might be objected that this is merely an intermediate generalisation, somewhere between the statement that 'She stole the coat' and the general statement that 'Women will do self-damaging things if they think that this will make their nearest and dearest concerned about them'. In a sense this may be so: but it would make perfectly good sense if a clinician were to say 'Other women may or may not behave like this when their spouses neglect them. I don't know and I don't care. What

[9] And not only individual human beings.

[10] Again, we may insert some word such as 'usually' and turn it into a statement of limited but imprecise applicability.

I can tell you is that *this one* does.' Alternatively, he might say 'I can make the general statement that *this* woman reacts like this to her husband's neglect of her. No doubt she is not unique and there are other women who react similarly to similar situations. But I do not have the information needed to define the category of women who do so.' There is no logical reason why a clinician should not formulate general statements which are 'idiosyncratic'—that is, apply only to the behaviour of a single patient. Indeed, really intelligent psychotherapists do tend to formulate idiosyncratic generalisations about the behaviour of individual patients.[11] To do so does not imply that the same statements could not be made about other people: only that the explainer is not in a position to make them about other people.

Mutatis mutandis, an idiosyncratic explanation can also be offered for the behaviour of a particular group of people, whether small or large. 'This is how the Scottish National Party react when . . .' is the beginning of an idiosyncratic probability-explanation. On the other hand, group-rates are not, for obvious reasons, the sort of explananda for which idiosyncratic explanations can be offered.

The main point of this chapter, however, is that what has to be decided by the explainer of any particular instance of unexpected behaviour is in the first place whether he has enough information to justify him in giving anything more than a possibility-explanation. Such information must include *either* similar behaviour by some class of people to which the actor can be assigned (e.g. women, or middle-aged married women) in a class of situations to which the situation in question can be assigned (e.g. neglect by husband) *or* similar behaviour by the particular actor in at least one other situation which can be regarded as similar.

---

[11] Although these generalisations sometimes turn into statements about 'types' of patient when the psychotherapist publishes a paper of takes part in a seminar.

13　The criminologist's stone

In the previous chapter I discussed Durkheim's principle of 'one effect, one cause' and undertook to illustrate what nonsense can be made of it by a failure to recognise it as nothing more than a fairly sound methodological rule. The best illustration is what I have called 'the criminologist's stone'.

This venerable landmark is the rallying-point of those positivist sociologists who have for the last century been at war with what is sometimes called 'the multifactorial approach' and sometimes simply 'multiple causation'. On the one side in this guerilla war are the field-workers who patiently glean data about the multiplicity of variables associated with different kinds of misbehaviour, bent over their calculating machines like peasants over their ploughs. Sniping at them from the heights are the glamorous partisans of unitary theory, believing either in some general explanation of all crime (and sometimes deviance to boot), or at least in the ultimate victory of such an explanation. For this is to some extent an ideological feud, in which the partisans are sustained by faith rather than by facts, the peasants by common sense rather than success.

The feud seems to have been started, as I have said, by Durkheim. In *The Rules of Sociological Method* he was attacking J. S. Mill's commonsense assumption that the same effect could be due sometimes to one cause, sometimes to another.

'This supposed axiom of the plurality of causes is, in fact, a negation of the principle of causality,' he wrote: a sentiment which was to be echoed by Cohen and Wilkins more than half a century later. The principle which Durkheim laid down was 'one effect, one cause'. In his case no great harm was done, because he reasoned that if, say, suicide was attributable to more than one cause, it was because there was more than one kind of suicide. 'The same is true of crime'. The trouble was partly that the principle itself was somewhat perfectionist, but chiefly that not all criminologists have reasoned from it to the common-sense and harmless conclusion that there must be more than one kind of crime. Instead, they have arrived at the incredible inference that there must be a single explanation of crime, if only it could be found and formulated.

It is worth noting that those who have reasoned in this way have all been sociologists. 'Grand theory' has the sort of prestige among sociologists of deviance which Grand Opera has in the world of singers. Durkheim's followers have included such well-known sociologists as Sutherland, Albert Cohen, Matza and Wilkins. Most, if not all, of them have been concerned to protect their own more or less monolithic object of worship, whether this was differential association,[1] delinquent value-systems, drift, or 'a general theory of deviance.'[2]

The targets of this guerilla warfare have usually been psychologists, such as Healy (1915) and Burt (1944). Very few sociologists have dared to question the monolithic approach, although Merton is an exception:

'. . . the assumption that a single theory will account for

---

[1] See Chapter 4 of the 8th edition of Sutherland and Cressey (1970).

[2] It is not quite clear how general Cohen or Matza intend their applica-tion of their own theories to be. Both were writing about young male delinquents, although Cohen does say 'If the explanation is sound, then the general theory should provide a key to the understanding of other subcultures as well. If the general theory does not fit other subcultures as well then the explanation of this particular subculture is thrown into question.' (1955: 50). Matza's *Delinquency and Drift* (1964) was written with young male delinquents in mind, and it is not entirely clear whether 'drift' is offered as a universal explanation. His later book, *Becoming Deviant* (1969) adds two other explanatory concepts, 'affiliation' and 'signification'. On the other hand, there is no doubt about Wilkins' intentions, for he calls his type of explanation 'A General Theory of Deviance' (1964, Ch. 4).

the entire range of behaviour placed in this category (sc. "crime or delinquency") . . . is not too remote, in logical structure, from the assumption of a Benjamin Rush . . . that there must be a theory of disease, rather than distinct theories of disease. . . . Just as classifying enormously varied conditions and processes under the one heading of disease led some zealous medical systematics to believe that it was their task to evolve a single over-arching theory of disease, so, it seems, the established idiom, both vernacular and scientific, of referring to "juvenile delinquency" as though it were a single entity, leads some to believe that there must be a basic theory of 'its' causation . . .' (1968 ed., p. 231).

But this was a cry in the wilderness. Even the Gluecks, who were so often the targets in this guerilla war, hesitated to renounce the idea of a single theory completely, although at first they questioned whether it was attainable:

'We regret that we are as yet not able to emerge with a single theory that will "explain" all delinquency and crime: and there is of course the question whether this will ever be possible in view of the "multitude of sins" and the varieties of acts. . . . We are searching for the relevant facts and will continue to do so, unimpeded, we hope, by the stranglehold of a vague, thin and cloudy unilateral "theory" of crime causation . . .' (p. 79).

Two years later, however, when they wrote the introduction to *Ventures in Criminology*, they seem to have succumbed to intimidation, or perhaps convinced themselves that at last they were within sight of the criminologists' stone:

'We hope that by a systematic, widely embracing process it will be possible to arrive at a unifying theory which will

integrate relevant information from both a constitutional
and a socio-cultural matrix. This may well provide a break-
through in the quest for definitive explanations of the
delinquency phenomenon.' (p. 9)

The search for the stone may seem a little passé nowadays: so
many megaliths have risen and fallen and so varied are the
types of conduct which they have purported to explain. There
is however nothing actually illogical about this optimism.
Indeed as Matza points out:

'theories should be elegant and parsimonious, and not
simply for reasons of aesthetic sensibility. . . . When
many factors matter rather than few, and no one can
pretend to know how many is too many, this may be a
signal that our model is not a truthful simplifying of
reality but instead a complicated falsehood.' (1964, p. 23).

This is a slightly arabesque version of Occam's razor, but none
the less sharp for that.
   Wolfgang and Ferracuti seem to regard heuristic considerations as paramount:

'. . . the basic issue is: which approach provides for greater
efficiency in the pursuit of adequate applicable knowledge
and *which is more consonant with a sound philosophy of
science* . . .' (p. 61).

Perhaps the most interesting part of this quotation, however,
is the clause which I have italicised. This implies that which-
ever of the two approaches—multiple causation or unitary
theory—is heuristically the more useful will also be more consonant with a sound philosophy of science. It would have been
interesting if the authors had followed up this remark by a

logical analysis of the case for and against multiple-factor approaches; but they did not, probably because they were intent on patching up a sort of peace treaty between the two sides.[3]

It is difficult to resist the impression, however, that the peacemakers are really monolith-seekers who are trying to practise the charitable maxim of *parcere subjectis*. Wolfgang and Ferracuti are by their own admission working towards an integrated theory. Hirschi and Selvin—who have done a great deal to clarify the notion of causation[4] in criminology—have contributed a most judicial and acute summing-up which has

[3] 'The two positions, when viewed in this perspective, are not, in fact, so far removed from one another that resolution of differences' is impossible. Multiple-factor adherents should:

1. state more explicitly the reasons for their 'choice' of particular items for analysis;
2. attempt to arrange these reasons for delimited factor choice within an integrated and meaningful relationship of factors, for factors that remain outside the framework of the rationale for selection are meaningless even if correlated with the dependent variable;
3. seek to link previous unintegrated but highly correlated data to existing theory; and
4. produce new theory which their integrated efforts may provide.

The generalizing theorists should:

1. examine and make more extensive use of analysis of data already collected by the multiple-factor approach in order to produce theory more closely linked to existing research;
2. specify more explicitly the range and parameters of their conceptualizations;
3. employ wherever possible the full complement of operational concepts in the theories so that data may be gathered to support the theories directly;
4. provide wherever possible operational hypotheses that flow directly from the general theory;
5. suggest the best sources and level of quantitative and qualitative data that could be used to examine the specific components of the theory' (op. cit. p. 62).

[4] Although they continue to talk, like Mill and Durkheim, in terms of 'causes', as to which see p. 8.

to be read with great care before it is apparent that they are at heart monolith-preservers:

> 'Now if researchers have erred in thinking that multiple causation makes an overall theory of delinquency untenable, theorists have erred in thinking that the idea of a single theory makes multiple causation untenable. The researcher who finds that there are "more than 170 distinct conditions . . . conducive to childish misconduct", is mistaken if he concludes that this number cannot be reduced by theoretical abstraction. The theorist who concludes that his two or three theoretical variables cannot be expanded to hundreds of distinct measures is also mistaken . . .' (p. 181: the quotation is from Burt).

There are some excellent points here. Many of the 'variables' which are listed by Healey, Burt and the Gluecks are really indices; that is, they are attempts to measure something which may contribute to delinquency, but which cannot be assessed directly. Thus Burt's 'mother deserted, separated or divorced' and his 'mother at work' were not so much independent variables as two indirect and crude measures of the adequacy of maternal supervision. In any case, even if they are regarded as variables in their own right, they can be 'abstracted' into 'adequacy of maternal supervision', which by a further abstraction can be combined with similar information about the father into 'quality of parental care'.

ECLECTICISM

An important distinction, however, is being overlooked. It is true

  (i) that a variable can be measured by more than one index;
  (ii) that a single explanatory statement can include more than one variable (as it does, for example, whenever it describes a set of sufficient conditions for the occurrence of an event).

But it is equally undeniable

(iii) that—to use the language of sufficient conditions[5]—there may be more than one set[6] of sufficient conditions for the occurrence of an event.

And it is perfectly reasonable—and consistent with (i) and (ii)—to hold

(iv) that not all sets of sufficient conditions can be linked to the event by the same scientific theory.

Thus in criminology there are commonsense peasants who will persist in assertions which take the following form:

(1) the explanation of some crimes is to be found in congenital defects, leading to difficulty in cognitive learning or sociali-sation;
(2) the explanations of others are to be found in faulty up-bringing;
(3) there are some crimes which cannot plausibly be explained in ways (1) or (2), but must be attributed to the influence of reference-groups;
(4) there are some crimes which cannot be explained in ways (1), (2) or (3), but must be attributed to sheer pressure of circumstances such as hunger, fear or the absence of legiti-mate car-parking space (whether or not my distinction be-tween possibility- and probability-explanations is accepted).

No conceivable process of abstraction could produce out of these a statement or set of statements that could plausibly be called a 'single' or 'integrated' theory. It would be possible of course to produce a summary of sorts, on the following lines: 'the incidence of crime is a function of congenital traits,

---

[5] Because it is the simplest though not the only terminology in which the point can be made.
[6] Different sets may of course have some but not all conditions in common: see p. 37n.

upbringing, reference-group values, opportunities and rational motivation'. But this is not a theory. It is what Homans rightly dismisses as a mere 'orienting' statement (see pp. 41–2) which tells us in what directions to look for relevant variables.

In short, it is when multifactorial approaches take what can be called an 'eclectic' form that the conflict with the integrated theory school becomes irreconcilable. Eclectism in this context means involving whatever body of theory seems to offer the most plausible explanation of a particular sub-group of 'crime'. It is really electicism which worries—or ought to worry—the monolith-seekers. So much so that the out-and-out monolith-seeker is not content with Occam's razor or weak heuristic arguments, but tries to discredit the eclectic by arguing that there is something logically or methodologically unsound about his position. This argument has not so far been clearly and fully stated, and it is therefore worthwhile to piece it together from the main sources.

Cohen's statement of it is to be found in his doctoral thesis:

'A multiple factor approach is not a theory; it is an abdication of the quest for a theory. It simply asserts that this particular event is "caused" by this particular combination of circumstances and that particular event by another combination of circumstances. [Cohen uses the term "factor" to mean "a particular concrete circumstance".] This delinquency is caused by "bad neighbourhood", "feeble-mindedness" and "drunken mother"; that delinquency is caused by "poverty", "broken home", "bad health" and "premature puberty" ...' (1951).

He makes it clear, however, that this does not exclude theories which involve a multiplicity of variables. A variable he describes as 'a logical universal . . . a characteristic or aspect with respect to which an object or event may vary, such as "velocity". . . . Values of the variable are logical particulars;

they are the logically possible different concrete circumstances which meet the criterion defining the variable, such as "30 miles per hour".' This makes a 'factor' in Cohen's sense sound rather like a particular value of a variable: but he is intent on distinguishing the two terms and does not discuss this. For he has to concede, of course, that there is nothing wrong with a theory which involves more than one variable. What he does insist upon is that

'Explanation calls not for a single factor but for a single theory or system of theory applicable to all cases. It is not the attendant circumstances but the demonstration that the event and the attendant circumstances are a special case of generalised theory which constitutes an explanation.' (ibid.)

Genuine single-factor theories are certainly rare. Henry VIII believed that idleness was 'mother and root of all vices . . . thefts, murders and other heinous offences and great enormities' (see the preamble to the statute 22, Henry VIII, c.12). In modern times the late Edward Glover believed that 'the unconscious need for punishment' was 'the key to all problems of delinquency' (p. 302). But what would constitute a 'single theory' in Cohen's eyes? As we have seen, it cannot be the use of not more than one 'variable'. But must it link together in one statement all the variables which it uses?

The point can be illustrated by considering what sort of explanation can be offered of cases in which vehicles overturn on roads. The ordinary motorist would probably be prepared to say that this happens either because they are knocked sideways by another vehicle or because they were struck by a strong wind or because they changed direction too quickly, or because an axle or some other part gave way. Any single statement which would embrace all these possibilities would obviously be a very complex one. To explain collisions one would have to describe the traffic system; to explain overturning in high winds one would need a bit of meteorology; to explain capsizing on bends one would have to talk about Newton's first law of motion (p. 52): to explain the failure of an axle one might have to drag in metallurgy and chemistry. This may be why Cohen is careful to say 'single theory or *system of theory*' (my italics), a phrase which would certainly allow of more than one statement using more than one set of concepts.

But what would then give it a claim to unity? What distinguishes a system from a collection? Cohen does not tell us; so that we may speculate. The minimum requirement is obviously consistency; no pair of theoretical statements could be regarded as part of the same system if they contradicted each other. This would allow a 'system' to consist of two or more non-contradictory explanations even if one were drawn from, say physics and the other from chemistry. This sort of eclecticism would be quite satisfactory for the common-sense criminologist, who would like to invoke psychiatry to explain some crimes, and learning theory, economics and perhaps culture-conflict to explain others.

But Cohen is certainly not preaching eclecticism: so what is he demanding? Probably that all the general statements should come from the same science. Just as one could conceivably ask that all the explanations of overturned vehicles should be drawn from physics, so might he be asking that all the explanations of crime should be drawn from, say psychology (or even from a branch of it, such as learning theory). After all this is what some of the major theorists—Sutherland (1947) and Eysenck being examples—have attempted. Nor are such attempts confined to criminology. Skinner and Homans (1961) for example, offer general theories to explain all forms of social behaviour.

But Cohen does not carry his argument further than the passage I have quoted, so that we are already within the realm of speculation. Are Wilkins or Matza more explicit?

Wilkins, writing in the middle sixties, is clearly a spiritual descendant of Durkheim, through Cohen. Durkheim regarded 'the supposed axiom of the plurality of causes' as a 'negation of the principle of causality'. Cohen labelled it 'an abdication of the quest for a theory'. Wilkins outdoes both when he says that it can hardly 'be dignified by the term "theory"' ... At best it must be considered an anti-theory which proposes that no theory can be formed regarding crime. (pp. 36–7).

A logician, however, could fairly point out that the multiple causation approach is neither a theory nor an anti-theory. It might conceivably be called a 'meta-theory', if it involved a categorical statement about theories. It is doubtful, however, whether it even does that. It would be more precise to call it (as Matza does) a 'principle': that is, a prescription for an approach to the problem of explanation. The principle could be stated in either a strong or a weak form. In the strong form it would be 'Plan your research on the assumption that there is no monolith to be found'. In a more moderate form it would be 'Plan it so that if there is no monolith to be found your work will not be wasted'.

It is this logical error which leads Wilkins to take up the extreme view that the multiple causation approach is in some way unscientific:

'Proponents of the theory would claim that since research has found no single factor as the cause of crime, but rather that many different factors appear together associated with greater or lesser frequency of criminal activity, this is evidence for multiple causation. But the theory does not facilitate the deduction of any hypotheses or practical consequences that are of any help whatsoever. If it is claimed that the theory applies to all factors which are operationally found to be related to criminal tendencies as they become known, it is apparent that the theory lacks the major and essential feature of any scientific theory—it is framed in such a way that it is impossible to find any test whereby it could be proved wrong.' (ibid., p. 37).

This is a very odd argument. Of course it is impossible to think of any test by which the principle could be proved wrong. To prove it wrong would be to prove the opposite: that is, that a 'single factor' is responsible for crime. Leaving aside any views one may have about the likelihood of this, what sort of 'test' would prove this? Only, I suggest, the actual discovery of some single 'factor' which could be shown to be a 'cause' of all crime; or at least could not be shown not to be. The alternative would be to devise some sort of proof in advance of any such discovery that there must be such a factor, which is hardly conceivable.

Matza's reasoning is more satisfactory (and incidentally leads to a less extreme view about the acceptability of what he calls 'multi-causation'). I have already quoted his sensible reminder about Occam's razor. He also has an interesting distinction to make, this time between factors and contingencies:

'When factors become too numerous, there is a tendency for them to be not factors at all, but rather contingencies. The term factor after all means something. A factor is a condition that is applicable to a given universe. It has an effect on everyone, not equally to be sure but according to degree. Factors may matter to varying extents, but every factor must by definition matter to some extent. Is the way in which a policeman responded to a child on their first meeting a factor? Does it matter or not? Is American foreign policy a factor? Does it matter or not? . . . And so on, endlessly. Common sense tells us that these occurrences may matter, or not, depending on many other things that may more legitimately be called factors. Some occurrences may or may not matter. Thus, they are contingencies and not factors . . .' (1964, pp. 22-3).

The point is worth making. But it will not reduce Burt's list very substantially; and hardly any of the Glueck's list can be dismissed as 'contingencies'. I doubt whether Matza himself regards this as a conclusive argument against the principle of multiple causation.

Where he does carry Cohen's argument a stage further is where he says:

> 'Whenever objections are raised about a specific viewpoint or more fundamental objections about the preconception of positive criminology, serious discussion and scrutiny is evaded by the seemingly frank and humble admission that "other factors are operative". The principle of multi-causation may be an honorable heuristic device. But it may also become a powerful force for intellectual inertia. It may point the way to new discoveries. Or it may allow discussants to dodge the necessity of a serious reappraisal of the nature of their object of study. Whether the principle of multi-causation is a legitimate heuristic device or *a way of avoiding the implications of negative evidence* depends, partially, on the number of factors invoked.' (ibid., p. 22; my italics).

The crucial clause in this passage is the one in which he points out that the notion of multiple causation may be 'a way of avoiding the implications of negative evidence'. This seems to me the clearest and most logical statement of the case against eclecticism, although Matza can hardly be said to have stated it in full in nine words. For the eclectic position, in its simplest form, is this:

> 'Some crimes are ascribable to cause A, some to cause B, some to cause C . . .' (and so on).

Thus, if evidence is produced to show that a particular crime is not ascribable to A, or that not all crimes of a certain category are ascribable to A, the eclectic can always say, 'Ah well, it (or some, as the case may be) must be ascribable to B or C'. It is this which gives the eclectic position the appearance of being incapable of falsification; and if Wilkins' objection had taken this form, rather than the more sweeping form which it did take, it would have been less easy to dispose of:

There does seem, however, to be a valid answer even to this formidable objection. So long as two conditions are fulfilled, it can be maintained that eclectic approaches are not unfalsifiable. The conditions are:

    1. that the eclectic's list of possible causes is a finite one: that is, that having named those which he can name he does not end up by saying, 'and so on' or words to that effect.
    2. that every one of his named possibilities is capable of being falsified empirically.

If these conditions are both fulfilled, then any given eclectic set of explanations is falsifiable.

At first sight, of course, these conditions appear to set an impossibly high standard. Must the eclectic show how each possible explanation could be falsified, given our present techniques of research? Or is it sufficient that it should be possible to imagine how each might be falsified? In short, is he being asked for practical or theoretical falsifiability? Karl Popper, to whom we owe the falsifiability criterion, would clearly answer 'theoretical falifiability'.[7]

By the same token, the eclectic can argue that so long as the list of causes which he has in mind is finite in nature, his position can be regarded as scientific (in Popper's sense) even if he cannot confidently say at this stage 'and that is the end of the list'. It might be reasonable, however, to ask of him that

---

[7] See K. R. Popper (1963, p. 39) 'The criterion of falsifiability . . . says that statements, or systems of statements, in order to be regarded as scientific, must be capable of conflicting with possible, *or conceivable*, observations' (my italics).

he should reach a point on his list at which he is prepared to say, 'and there are some other causes, but the crimes attributable to them are negligible in number'. This would give his opponent the chance of pointing to a category of crimes which was not negligible in number, and could not be explained by anything on the eclectic's list. That particular list would then be shown to be defective, although the eclectic peasant could then get down to work in the hope of unearthing the missing explanations.

In this discussion I have had to include a rather large collection of quotations in order to show that not only Durkheim but also several contemporary sociologists with high and deserved reputations really have expressed the views which I have been dissecting. But here is one final quotation—this time from a philosopher—which I include for the sheer love of it:

> 'There was once a man who aspired to be the author of the general theory of holes. When asked "What kind of hole—holes dug by children in the sand . . . holes dug by gardeners . . . tank traps, holes made by roadmakers?" he would reply indignantly that he wished for a general theory that would explain all of these. He rejected *ab initio* the . . . pathetically commonsense view that of the digging of different holes there are quite different kinds of explanation to be given; why then, he would ask, do we have the concept of a hole? . . .'

MacIntyre was in fact writing about political science, but he could well have been parodying general theories of deviance.

K

Summary

It may help the ordinary reader (not to mention the hard-pressed student or reviewer) if I summarise the main points made in the preceding chapters, but deliberately shuffling them so as to emphasise connections in a way which cannot be done by mere cross-referencing.

The instrumentalist's insistence that an explanation must help in predicting, producing or preventing something is too sweeping. By doing this an explanation increases our confidence in it; but it is not an essential function of an explanation. What is essential is that it answers a 'Why?' question in a way that to some extent satisfies the questioner's curiosity. This means that in the last resort it is for the questioner to say whether the explanation is complete enough to satisfy him; but there are objective tests which it must pass, and if it passes them he cannot reject it without giving sensible reasons.

By the same token, it is the questioner's curiosity which must provide at least the provisional definition of the explanandum, and not any demarcation dispute about the boundaries of disciplines, such as criminology and the sociology of deviance. The provisional definition, however, sometimes has to be revised in the light of the explanation, which may explain more or less than the originally defined explanandum. Even so, discipline-boundaries are still irrelevant. In the case of human actions the definition of the explanandum must always include the actor's state of mind and when it is refined in this way the questioner may *or may not* cease to feel that an explanation is necessary.

Nevertheless, the assumption that the ideal explanation is

scientific in form is out of date. It is true that we rightly reject several other kinds of explanation—'What-explanations' and final or formal causes. But that does not leave us with nothing but scientific explanations. If, as is argued, the essence of a scientific explanation is not its logical structure—as Hempel and others assume—but the fact that it is intended to tell the questioner why the explanandum was *inevitable or highly probable*, then there is clearly another kind of explanation which we regularly accept: the 'narrative' kind, which merely tells why the explanandum was *not impossible*.

It is the narrative explanation, rather than 'understanding', which should take over part of the territory from scientific explanations, especially in the field of human behaviour. Explanations of the scientific type are neither asked for nor appropriate to many explananda as defined by questioners' curiosity. They are appropriate only where the explanandum is a *regularity* in occurrences. In the field of human behaviour this regularity may consist of group-rates or individual tendencies and may be instances of known classes of such tendencies or may may be idiosyncratic; i.e., the only known case of such a tendency.

Since scientific explanations however are concerned with occurrences of high probability, they are less often appropriate to instances of misbehaviour than to instances of behaviour, that is, of expected as distinct from unexpected behaviour. Rule-breaking[1] and other surprising behaviour is, by its nature, likely to be susceptible only of a narrative explanation, although there are plenty of exceptions.[2] Sociology, psychology, economics or politics will often be able to tell us that certain *necessary* conditions for this or that kind of misbehaviour are present or absent at certain times or places; but they will seldom be able to tell us when *all* the *sufficient* conditions will be present, and it will be left to a narrative to tell how this *can* happen. In

---

[1] I am of course not implying that all rule breaking is surprising.
[2] For example, misbehaviour of a chronic kind.

contrast, rule-following or other unsurprising behaviour is *ipso facto* probable behaviour, again with exceptions.[3]

Scientific explanations enable us to see occurrences as inevitable or highly probably by labelling them as instances of a special kind of generalisation which is called a law. A law differs from a merely enumerative generalisation in that the latter simply tells us what has been found to be the case in all or most known instances, whereas a law implies some ground for expecting the generalisation to hold good in future or hypothetical situations. This ground cannot be merely a neat mathematical description; it must consist of a mechanism or failing that an analogy. An analogy tells us that in some respects the phenomena obey the generalisation *as if* such and such mechanism were in operation, but without guaranteeing that they do so in every respect (if it did so it would be claiming the status of a mechanism).

Generalisations which are enumerative can be confirmed by inspection of what they enumerate. Generalisations which claim to be laws cannot be confirmed, merely subjected to attempts to disconfirm them by creating experimental situations in which negative instances could occur: those which survive such attempts command increased confidence. Mechanisms can be confirmed only by observations, which is possible only if 'observation' is interpreted in a fairly wide sense. In the case of analogies we do not look for confirmation or disconfirmation, merely for limitations. Simulation of human behaviour by computers or otherwise is essentially the construction of analogies.

The social sciences have great difficulty in substituting mechanisms for analogies, and are likely to continue to have this difficulty unless they are less snobbish about introspectibles —motives, reasons and such-like. This snobbery originated in a preference for publicly observable kinds of behaviour as objects of study, and for explanatory models which used precise but

---

[3] For example, breaches of traffic laws, or private breaches of codes prohibiting such things as nose-picking.

theoretical constructs rather than inaccurately reported experiences; but it has received support from the view of some modern philosophers that reasons and motives cannot be causes. It seems paradoxical however to reject as mechanisms of causation the only kind of causation which we can directly experience. Fortunately the arguments for doing so are not unanswerable; and in any case the question is not so much whether reasons etc., can be causes—a rather dated question—as whether they help us to see why some actions are highly probable, as of course they often do.

If all this is accepted, either because it is convincing or simply in order to see where the argument leads, where does it lead in fact? Certainly not to the complete abandonment of the scientific approach to human behaviour. Quite apart from the fact that science includes description as well as explanation, there seems to be no sort of behaviour for which it never makes sense to seek a probability-explanation: not even actions. Often a possibility-explanation is all we want, or all we have any hope of getting: but an action is not by its nature incapable of a probability-explanation. Even when it was contrary to a rule or an expectation we may ask why it was probable. Before doing so we should of course have some grounds—such as repetitiveness—for talking about probability rather than possibility. And we should be prepared to be told, sometimes, that the explainer cannot accept our grounds for seeking a probability-explanation. Where we see repetition he may see important differences. What the argument should lead to of course is fewer requests for probability-explanations of irregular behaviour and so, from a practical point of view, less optimism about the reduction of law-breaking and other misbehaviour by 'tackling causes'. And whether or not the distinction between the two kinds of explanation is accepted, the quest for a general theory which will account for all instances of crime or deviance or misbehaviour makes no more sense than would a search for a general theory of disease.

References

Whatever notation is used, references in a text interfere with smooth reading. In fact they are usually redundant, in the sense that the mere name of the author enables the publication to be found in the References. This is why in the text of this book author's names are only occasionally followed by dates—i.e. when these are necessary to distinguish two authors of the same name, two publications by the same author or two editions of the same publication.

ADLER, M. J. (1938) see MICHAEL, J. (1938).

ADVISORY COUNCIL ON THE PENAL SYSTEM (1974) *Young Adult Offenders*: (Chairman Sir Kenneth Younger) H.M.S.O., London.

ANDERSON, A. R. & MOORE, O. K. (1967) 'Models and explanations in the behavioral sciences' in *Concepts, theory and explanation in the behavioral sciences* (ed. G. J. Direnzo) Random House, New York.

ARGYLE, M. (1969) *Social Interaction*, Methuen, London.

AYER, A. J. (1967) 'Man as a Subject of Science' in *Philosophy, Politics and Society* (edd. P. Laslett and W. Runciman) Blackwell, Oxford.

BECKER, H. (1963) *Outsiders: studies in the sociology of deviance*, Free Press, New York.

BENNETT, J. H. (ed.) (1965) *Experiments in Plant Hybridisation: Mendel's original paper in English translation with commentary and assessment by the late Sir Ronald Fisher* . . . Oliver and Boyd, Edinburgh.

BONGER, W. A. (1936) *Introduction to Criminology* (English tr. by E. VanLoo from Dutch edition of 1933) Methuen, London.

BRAITHWAITE, R. B. (1946) 'Teleological Explanation' in *Proceedings of the Aristotelian Society*, 1946–7.
and see RAMSEY, F. P. (1931).

BROAD, C. D. (1937) *The Mind and its Place in Nature*, Kegan Paul, London.

BURT, C. (1925) *The Young Delinquent*, University of London Press, London.

CATLIN, G. (1937) 'The delimitation and measurability of political phenomena' in *American Political Science Review 21*. 255ff.
and see DURKHEIM, E. (1895).

CLARK, A. C. (1969) see DINITZ, S. (1969)

COHEN, A. K. (1951) 'Multiple Factor Approaches' in *Juvenile Delinquency and the Social Structure*, unpublished Ph.D. thesis, Harvard University, extract reproduced in *The Sociology of Crime and Delinquency*, ed. Wolfgang, Savitz and Johnson, New York, John Wiley & Sons, 1962 (2nd. ed. 1970).

COHEN, A. K. (1955) *Delinquent Boys*, Glencoe Free Press, New York.

COHEN, A. K. (1959) 'Social Disorganisation and Deviant Behaviour' in *Sociology Today*, ed. R. K. Merton, Fress Press, Glencoe, Illinois.

COHEN, S. (1973) 'The Failures of Criminology' in *The Listener*, 8 November, pp. 622ff.

COLBY, K. (1975) *Artificial Paranoia*, Pergamon, New York, Oxford.

CRESSEY, D. R. (1953) *Other People's Money*, Free Press, Glencoe, Illinois.
and see SUTHERLAND, E. H. and CRESSEY, D. R. (1970).

DINITZ, S., DYNES, R. R. & CLARK, A. C. (1969) *Deviance: studies in definition, management and treatment*, Oxford University Press, London.

DOLLARD, J., MILLER, N. et al. (1939) *Frustration and Aggression*, Yale University Press, Newhaven.

DOOB, A. L. (1968) see FREEDMAN, J. L. (1968).

DOUGLAS, J. D. (1972) 'The absurd and the problem of social order' in *Theoretical Perspectives on Deviance* (edd. R. A. Scott and J. D. Douglas) Basic Books, New York.

DRAY, W. (1957) *Laws and Explanations in History*, Oxford University Press, London.

DURKHEIM, E. (1895) *The Rules of Sociological Method* (1950 tr. Solovay, S, and Mueller, J: ed. Catlin, G.) Free Press, Glencoe, Illinois.

DYNES, R. R. (1969) see DINITZ, S. (1969)

EYSENCK, H. J. (1964) *Crime and Personality*, Routledge, London.

FREEDMAN, J. L. & DOOB, A. L. (1968) *Deviancy: the psychology of being different*, Academic Press, New York.

GARFINKEL, H. (1967) *Studies in Ethnomethodology*, Prentice-Hall, Englewood Cliffs, New Jersey.

GLOVER, E. (1964) *The Roots of Crime: Selected Papers on Psycho-Analysis*, 2, International Universities Press, New York.

GLUECK, S. and E. (1962) & (1964) 'Family environment and delinquency in the perspective of etiologic research'. Paper presented at the XII International Congress in Criminology, Hebrew University. Reproduced in their *Ventures in Criminology*, London, Tavistock, 1964.

GOFFMAN, E. (1963) *Stigma: notes on the management of spoiled identity*, Prentice-Hall, Englewood Cliffs, New Jersey.

HARRÉ, R. (1972) *The Philosophy of Science*, Oxford University Press, London.

HARRÉ, R. & SECORD, P. (1972) *The Explanation of Social Behaviour*, Blackwell, Oxford.

HART, H. L. A. & HONORÉ, A. M. (1959) *Causation in the Law*, Clarendon Press.

HEALEY, W. (1915) *The Individual Delinquent*, Little, Brown & Co., Boston.

HEMPEL, C. G. (1965) *Aspects of Scientific Explanations: and other essays within the philosophy of science*. Free Press, New York.

HESSE, M. (1970) *Models and Analogies in Science*, University of Notre Dame Press, Notre Dame, Indiana.

HIRSCHI, T. and SELVIN, H. (1967) *Delinquency Research: An Appraisal of Analytic Methods*, Free Press, New York.

HOMANS, G. C. (1961) *Social Behaviour: its elementary forms* Routledge and Kegan Paul, London.

HOMANS, G. C. (1967) *The Nature of Social Science*, Harcourt, Brace & World, New York.

KITSUSE, (1962) 'Societal reactions to deviant behaviour: problems of theory and method' in *Social Problems*, 9, 4, 247ff.

KUHN, T. S. (1962) *The Structure of Scientific Revolutions*, University of Chicago Press.

LEMERT, E. M. (1951) *Social Pathology*, McGraw-Hill, New York.

LEMERT, E. M. (1969) *Human Deviance, Social Problems and Social Control*, Prentice-Hall, Englewood Cliffs, New Jersey.

LUKES, S. (1970) 'Methodological Individualism Reconsidered' in *Social Theory and Philosophical Analysis*, (edd. Emmet, D. & MacIntyre, A.) Macmillan, London.

MACINTYRE, A. (1971) *Against the Self-Images of the Age*, Duckworth, London.

MACIVER, R. M. (1950) *The Ramparts we Guard*, Macmillan, New York.

MANNHEIM, H. (1965) *Comparative Criminology*, (2 vols) Routledge and Kegan Paul, London.

MATZA, D. (1964) *Delinquency and Drift*, John Wiley, New York, London.

MATZA, D. (1969) *Becoming Deviant*, Prentice-Hall, Englewood Cliffs, New Jersey.

McCORD, W. and J. & ZOLA, I. K. (1959) *Origins of Crime*, Columbia University Press, New York.

MEEHAN, E. J. (1968) *Explanation in Social Science: a system paradigm*. Dorsey Press, Homewood, Illinois.

MERTON, R. (1938) 'Social Structure and Anomie' in *American Sociological Review*, 3, 677–82.

MERTON, R. (1949) *Social Theory and Social Structure*, Free Press, Glencoe, Illinois. (revised ed. 1968).

MICHAEL, J. & ADLER, M. J. (1938) *Crime, Law and Social Science*, New York.

MILLER, N. E. (1939) see DOLLARD, J. (1939)

MILLS, C. W. (1943) 'The Professional Ideology of Social Pathologists' in *American Journal of Sociology*, 49, 165ff.

NETTLER, G. (1957) 'A Measure of Alienation' in *American Sociological Review*, 22, p. 670.

PACKER, H. (1969) *The Limits of the Criminal Sanction*. Stanford University Press, Stanford.

PETERS, R. S. (1958) *The Concept of Motivation*, Routledge and Kegan Paul, London.

PHILLIPSON, M. (1971) *Sociological Aspects of Crime and Delinquency*, Routledge and Kegan Paul, London.

POPPER, K. R. (1963) *Conjectures and Refutations*, Routledge and Kegan Paul, London.

RAMSEY, F. P. (1931) *The Foundation of Mathematics*, (ed. R. B. Braithwaite) Kegan Paul, London.

REISS, A. (1964) 'An Empirical Test of Differential Association' in *Journal of Research in Crime and Delinquency, I*, 1: 5ff.

RICKMAN, H. P. (1967) *Understanding and the Human Studies*, Heinemann, London.

RIESMAN, D., GLAZER, N. & DENNEY, R. (1950) *The Lonely Crowd*, Yale University Press, New Haven.

RYAN, A. (1970) *The Philosophy of the Social Sciences*, Macmillan, London.

RYAN, A. (1973) *The Philosophy of Social Explanation*, Oxford University Press, London.

SARBIN, T. R. and MILLER, J. E. (1970) 'Demonism revisited: the XYY chromosome analogy' in *Issues in Criminology*.

SELLIN, T. (1938) *Culture, Conflict and Crime*, Social Science Research Council Bulletin 41, New York.

SCHEFF, T. (1966) *Being Mentally Ill: a sociological theory.* Weidenfeld & Nicholson, London.

SCRIVEN, M. (1962) 'Explanations, Predictions and Laws' in *Minnesota Studies in the Philosophy of Science*, (ed. R. Feigl) *3*, p. 190.

SKINNER, B. F. (1971) *Beyond Freedom and Dignity*, Jonathan Cape, London.

SROLE, L. (1956) 'Social Integration and certain corollaries: an Exploratory Study' in *American Sociological Review, 21*, p. 709.

SUTHERLAND, E. H. (1947) *Principles of Criminology*, Lippincott, Philadelphia. (later editions jointly with D. R. CRESSEY: see e.g. SUTHERLAND, E. H. and CRESSEY, D. R. 1970)

SUTHERLAND, E. H. and CRESSEY, D. R. (1970) 'A sociological theory of criminal behaviour' in *Criminology*, 8th ed., Lippincott, Philadelphia. (for original edition see SUTHERLAND, E. H., (1947).

TAYLOR, D. M. (1970) *Explanation and Meaning*, Cambridge University Press, Cambridge.

TAYLOR, I., WALTON, P. & YOUNG, J. (1973) *The New Criminology*, Routledge and Kegan Paul, London.

TOULMIN, S. (1953) *The Philosophy of Science: an Introduction*, Hutchinson's University Library, London.

WALKER, N. D. (1957) *A Short History of Psychotherapy*, Routledge and Kegan Paul, London.

WALKER, N. D. (1965) *Crime and Punishment in Britain*, Edinburgh University Press.

WALTON, P. see TAYLOR, I. (1973)

WILKINS, L. (1964) *Social Deviance: Social Policy, Action and Research*, London, Tavistock.

WILLER, D. (1967) *Scientific Sociology*, Prentice-Hall, Englewood Cliffs, New Jersey.

WILSON, B. (ed.) (1970) *Rationality*, Blackwell, Oxford.

WINCH, P. (1958) *The Idea of a Social Science and its Relation to Philosophy*, Routledge and Kegan Paul, London.

WOLFGANG, M. and FERRACUTI, F. (1967) *The Subculture of Violence: Towards an Integrated Theory in Criminology*, Tavistock, London.

VON WRIGHT, G. H. (1971) *Explanation and Understanding*, Routledge and Kegan Paul, London.

YOUNG, J. (1971) *The Drug Takers*, MacGibbon and Kee, London.

YOUNG, J. (1971) 'The Role of the Police as Amplifiers of Deviancy, Negotiators of Reality and Translators of Fantasy' in S. Cohen (ed.) *Images of Deviance*, Harmondsworth, Penguin Books.

YOUNG, J. (1973) see TAYLOR, I, (1973)

YOUNGER, K. (1974) see ADVISORY COUNCIL ON THE PENAL SYSTEM (1974)

Index